MW01168989

Cadence

2024

FLORIDA STATE
POETS ASSOCIATION

Palm Paradise   by Nancy K. Hauptle MacInnis

Cadence
2024

FLORIDA STATE
POETS ASSOCIATION
ANTHOLOGY #42

Published by
Florida State Poets Association
Book design by
Marc Davidson, Bah, Humbug! Productions

Edited by
Sonja Jean Craig
Elaine Person
Mary Marcelle
Mark Andrew James Terry
Marc Davidson

Copyright 2024 © Florida State Poets Association, Inc.

Each poet retains individual copyright of their poems
appearing in this anthology. All rights reserved.

ISBN # 9798341065680

Printed in the United States of America

www.floridastatepoetsassociation.org

Cover Photographs

Front

Winter Park Boat Tour
Cheryl Lynn West

Back

Light of Love
Juliana Romnes

Table of Contents

Orlando Area Poets (cont.)

Poetry For The Love Of It

Space Coast Poets

FSPA Members-At-Large (cont.)

FSPA CONTEST WINNERS

FSPA CONTEST WINNERS (cont,)

Introduction

It is with grateful privilege that I introduce this collection of poems – the 42nd Edition of *Cadence,* the Florida State Poets Association Anthology. This book is a time-honored tradition to showcase the vast talent of our members, most of whom are Florida poets, although we have extended our membership nationally. The first section is the work of our Chancellors, the pillars of poetry in Florida. The Chancellors stand for excellence from diverse perspectives. They work hard to bring poetry awareness to residents of Florida.

The *meat* of the collection features our members. They represent chapters from all over Florida as well as members at large nationally. Each poem was carefully selected by judges Elaine Person, Mark Andrew James Terry, and Mary Marcelle. I acknowledge them with admiration.

This is followed by contest winners from our annual contests. A selection of prompts was the inspiration for the innovative interpretations of poets worldwide and winners chosen by a team of anonymous judges. Thank you to Marc Davidson who organized the contest. I thank Marc, also, for his layout skills that brought this anthology to life.

The images that make up the cover and interior of the book were selected from our members. Their inspiration was "Heartscapes of Florida." We are blessed with multi-talented artists who added their photographic visions to the book.

Every part of *Cadence* is poetry, not only the poems, but the creative process and the finished book that you hold. Let these pages inspire fresh ideas and evoke feelings.

It is with pride that we created *Cadence 2024,* the 42nd edition of the Florida State Poets Association Anthology.

Sonja Jean Craig, *Cadence* Editor

O for a Muse of fire, that would ascend
The brightest heaven of invention,
A kingdom for a stage, princes to act
And monarchs to behold the swelling scene!
...But pardon, gentles all...
And let us, ciphers to this great accompt,
On your imaginary forces work...
Think when we talk of horses, that you see them
Printing their proud hoofs i' the receiving earth;
For 'tis your thoughts that now must deck our kings,
Carry them here and there; jumping o'er times,
Turning the accomplishment of many years
Into an hour-glass: for the which supply,
Admit me Chorus to this history;
Who prologue-like your humble patience pray,
Gently to hear, kindly to judge, our play.

William Shakespeare
— *King Henry V, Prologue*

FSPA Chancellors

Claire at Matanzas Inlet   by Catherine St. Jean

Silvia Curbelo

TROPICS

Summer's own backyard,
its long goodbye, trees heavy
with birds, no wind and
the temperature rising.
Heat like grief in the body,
the animal taste of it, metal
and salt, the air in free fall.
Thick clouds in the distance
ticking like piano notes
and random music everywhere,
a secret language in the dirt,
love or sex, some reckless
kind of beauty in abundance
like that underwater dream
I once had when we were young
and the silence was new
and the river owned us.

Denise Duhamel

POEM IN WHICH I MARRIED YOUNG AND STAYED IN MY HOME TOWN

I never became a poet because, well, who has time?
It was a kiddish, indulgent dream—I know that now.
Each morning I read The Academy of American Poets'
poem-a-day in my inbox, and honestly, I only understand
about a third of them. I hate pretense and obscure
mythology almost as much as I hated being married.
I was a restless bride and soon started catting around.
My husband divorced me when other wives called me
the town slut. But in their whispers I heard a tinge
of envy. I let my husband have the kids. I know—
what kind of mother does that? A mother
who thought she wanted to be a poet. A mother
who thought she had big pronouncements to make.
My journals were full of scribbles about life
and my longings. I even had a few verses published
and learned the hard way poets don't make
any money. So I went to school for cosmetology
and opened my very own beauty parlor called
Her Kind, named after the Anne Sexton poem.
I poured my ambition into gel manicures, eyebrow
threading, waxing and highlights. What, you might ask,
were the highlights of my life? Transforming brides
and their wedding parties on early mornings,
right in their homes, my assistant with mimosas
and the spray tan machine. Most townspeople
have forgotten or forgiven my own transgressions.
I can make the ugliest woman feel beautiful, move her
to tears. The way a poem sometimes still moves me.

Carol Frost

DEAD MAN'S BEDROOM

As a photo stops the brook from running
but keeps the brook bed and water after
severest drought, night's light – a multitude
of vanishing stars – streams through the window
of the dead man's bedroom and animates
his face. Though stilled past weariness.
One eye is closed, the other eye staring
deeply into the molecules of air,
bureau, doorframe, and someone standing there?
Who could know what he last saw or heard? Who?
But the raptness of his gaze as a sound
is like the owl's utterance from dark branch
and deep wood, is like the rush of water,
silence of stars that, once heard, says never
of what it is but what it is, ever.

Barbara Hamby

ODE TO FORGETTING THE YEAR

Forget the year, the parties where you drank too much,
      said what you thought without thinking, danced so hard
you dislocated your hip, fainted in the kitchen,
      while Gumbo, your host's Jack Russell terrier,
looked you straight in the eye, bloomed into a bodhisattva,
      lectured you on the six perfections while drunk people
with melting faces gathered around your shimmering corpse.

Then there was February when you should have been decapitated
      for stupidity. Forget those days and the ones when you
faked a smile so stale it crumbled like a cookie down the side
      of your face. Forget the crumbs and the mask you wore
and the tangle of Scotch tape you used to keep it in place,

but then you'd have to forget spring with its clouds of jasmine,
      wild indigo, and the amaryllis with their pink and red
faces, your garden with its twelve tomato plants, squash, zucchini,
      nine kinds of peppers, okra, and that disappointing row
of corn. Forget the corn, its stunted ears and brown oozing tips.
      Forgive the worms that sucked their flesh like zombies
and forgive the bee that stung your arm, then stung your face, too.

While we're at it, let's forget 1974. You should have died
      that year, or maybe you did. Resurrection's a trick
you learned early. And 2003. You could have called in sick
      those twelve months—sick and silly, illiterate and numb,

and summer, remember the day at the beach when the sun
        began to explain Heidegger to you while thunderclouds
rumbled up from the horizon like Nazi submarines? The fried
        oysters you ate later at Angelo's were a consolation and
the margaritas with salt and ice. Remember how you begged the
        sullen teenaged waitress
to bring you a double, and double that, pleasepleaseplease.

And forget all the crime shows you watched,
        the DNA samples, hair picked up with tweezers
and put in plastic bags, the grifters, conmen, and the husbands
        who murdered their wives for money or just plain fun.
Forget them and the third grade and your second boyfriend,
        who loved *Blonde on Blonde* as much as you did
but wanted something you wouldn't be able to give anyone
        for years.

Forget movies, too, the Hollywood trash in which nothing
        happened though they were loud and fast, and when they
were over time had passed, which was a blessing in itself.
        O blessed is Wong Kar Wai and his cities of blue and rain.
Blessed is David Lynch, his Polish prostitutes juking
        to *Locomotion* in a kitschy fifties' bungalow. Blessed
is Jeff Buckley, his *Hallelujah* played a thousand times in your
        car as you drove through Houston, its vacant lots
exploding with wild flowers and capsized shopping carts.

So forget the pizzas you ate, the ones you made from scratch
        and the Dominoes ordered in darkest December,
the plonk you washed it down with and your Christmas tree
        with the angel you found in Naples and the handmade
Santas your sons brought home from school, the ones with
        curling eyelashes and vampire fangs. Forget their heart-
breaks and your sleepless nights like gift certificates from the
        Twilight Zone, because January's here, and the stars are
singing a song you heard on a street corner once so wild the
        pavement rippled, and it called you like the night calls
you with his monsters and his marble arms.

19

Lola Haskins

A FIELD IN SPRING

*In Japanese ink-painting, the mantis body stroke is used
to render the point at which blades of grass widen.*

The painter slashes mantises

across the page.   But when

he turns and walks away

it is not the field that remains.

It is his gestures in the air.

From *Like Zeros, Like Pearls* (poems about insects), forthcoming
in early 2025 from Charlotte Lit Press.

David Kirby

WE THINK OTHER PEOPLE KNOW A WHOLE LOT MORE THAN WE DO BUT THEY DON'T

When I lived in Washington I was walking
through Lafayette Park one day and noticed
        this beautiful tree with a plaque on it that read
Liriodendrum tulipfera or tulip tree, so every time
        I was with someone else and we walked by
that or any other tulip tree and they remarked
        on what a beautiful tree it was, I'd say,

"Just a second . . . yeah, I think that's a tulip tree.
Liriodendrum tulipfera, right?" and they'd say,
        "Wow, you know Latin?" The answer to that
would be no: I took a year in high school
        a year in college, then gave it up, having come
to the same conclusion as top-shelf German poet,
        writer, and literary critic Heinrich Heine,

who said, "If the Romans had been obliged
to learn Latin, they would never have found time
        to conquer the world," a hypothesis that suggests
that maybe the Romans had to learn Latin
        because they started out speaking some other
language, like, I don't know, Japanese?
        Although a more realistic guess would be

that Heine didn't do all that well in his Latin classes
at Düsseldorf High—go, Lions! There I'm sure
        he studied the Archimedean solids, that is, the 13
convex polyhedra described by Archimedes
        in proofs that were lost sometime in the third
century BC but then reconstructed 1,800 years later
        by Heinrich Heine's countryman Johannes Kepler.

Okay, pay attention, because here is where it gets
tricky. The first widely disseminated discussion
        of Kepler's findings appeared in Lorenzo Mascheroni's
Geometria del Compasso of 1797, which is where
        the matter stood until 1928, when a student browsing
a rack of books in a Copenhagen bookshop found
        a book by Georg Mohr called *Euclides Danicus* (1672)

        that actually predated Mascheroni by more than
a hundred years. Here's the problem, though:
        Mohr's book was written in Danish. At that time,
the scientific lingua franca was, that's right, Latin,
        so had Mohr written in that language, anyone
interested in his findings would have been able to
        read him in Latin and credit Mohr with rediscovering

        Archimedes a hundred years before Mascheroni did.
But in Danish? Not going to happen. Eventually
        Mohr's book was translated into German and French,
but today even those languages have been replaced
        globally by English: you know that French doesn't
stand a chance these days when you realize that even
        French diplomats negotiate in English now, whereas,

        for centuries, French was the standard for international
diplomacy. So what will eventually replace English?
        Chinese, sure, but for how long? Guy down the street
has this theory that the earth is really a penal colony
        run by aliens, so if life forms from Pluthor are in charge,
does that mean eventually we'll all be speaking
        Pluthorian? Stranger things have happened—

        wait, no, they haven't, but a lot of strange things
have happened, like when inventor Thomas Midgley, Jr.
        came up with a compound called tetraethyl lead,
which, when added to gasoline, solved one of
        the biggest problems the automotive industry faced
at the time: engine knocking, or tiny explosions
        in car engines that resulted in an annoying sound

and potential damage. Okay, we all know what
lead does to human beings, especially children,
            but did you know that Midgley would go on
to leave his mark in history with a second destructive
            invention when he replaced the flammable gases
in air conditioners with chlorofluorocarbons
            that are harmless to humans yet deadly to

            the ozone layer? The planet is still recovering from
the ill effects of both inventions: leaded gasoline
            was sold in parts of the world until 2021,
and the ozone layer will need another four decades
            to heal fully, and many continue to live with
the long-term effects of lead poisoning. Hitler wanted
            to be a bad guy. Trump, Mussolini, Pol Pot:

            they were all bad guys and were proud of it.
But Midgely was trying to do good in the world
            and was hailed as a hero for decades. When
I lived in Washington and walked by a tulip tree
            with my friends and said, "Isn't that a *Liriodendrum
tulipfera*?" they thought I knew everything
            about another subject, too, which is botany.

M.B. McLatchey

ILLUMINATOR
for Geoffrey

In a light that you seem to trace
you see it now, its tangled shape:
a name poem like a nocturnal vine
started in school, but meant to flower –
to burst into bloom – at home.

Vowels already ablaze in carmine red
and verdigris. Glottal stops
that coil and link and knot
like tendrils finding their way
across a pleated page.

A manuscript of lists like canon tables
drawn in your own hand to answer
*Who is Geoffrey? G for gorgeous, great
athlete.* A fourth-grader's bravado, a pose
that I want to tell you

monks in your hunched position resisted
because they knew – alone in the listening night –
that the paint was theirs; theirs to make a pageant
of their own devotions, and not to bring new luster
to the daily rote of living.

And yet, your good apprenticeship
apparent in this trailing vine of watercolors,
apparent in this homely frame of references.
E, the wild look you see in your brother's face
and in the world: *Everything* girls want.

And how you beat us at our game
of self-display: lover of *Ostriches* and *Obelisks*.
Letters like ivied fences there to please.
Lists like crumbling columns of interior scenes
set into a folio of folding screens

that open – not to the ones who come to see
but to the screen maker who casts himself
along a linear leaf and works as servants do:
illuminator in his quiet cell; fold by fold,
changed by the paint as well.

Sean Sexton

MOMENT

And then one morning you rise in that same hour
and by the dismal room tell the next season has
has arrived—an imperceptible tide of darkness
has crept in. See it elsewise on sweated windows
of the library obscuring the pasture beyond,

closing the room into its own capsule of effects.
And there's already been a quieting as the wind
begins its measured halt, valves closing somewhere
as if something is saving up for storms of latter days
as an elderly couple might store their affection for sex.

Soon more change—air not exactly chill, but a
thinning one comes to know in the tropics. A swing
of time makes it so as life comes along in tow and we,
siblings of its spin—akin to the world's own death—
are along for the ride with no other way to go.

Virgil Suárez

RAILYARD AT DUSK

Behemoth against the burnt sienna
sky, metal ground to a halt, immense
millipede of blemished cars lined

into a vanishing horizon. Constant
hunger for clean air, acid rain pelts
the earth in a Morse code for the dead.

These trains stopped running long ago,
in another time when bridging distance
seemed like a good idea until we poisoned

the well. The pigeon carcasses lay strewn
on the roofs. We've killed everything
in our waking. We wipe our eyes as if

somehow all of it can start again,
but it is too late, or too soon for how
we consume every morsel strewn

by an invisible God hell bent on destruction.

FSPA Chapters
and Their Poets

Distant Gathering at Daytona Beach   by Juliana Romnes

Ancient City Poets

Patia Carque

WINTER

Wind stormed the door with a dusting of
dread, the ear of her soul heard a groan.
Winter has come to your home

Mourn spring mornings of yellow, blue blooms
body awakened to lilacs. His touch a promise
of life undenied, his punch a buried silence.

Scrumptious summer, luscious fruits steamed
quenching the thirst of her body in heat
bruised before life juices dried.

Orange golds, autumn reds blaze
as sunsets fade. Grief tree releasing
one last leaf, bending in barren surrender.

Winter has come to her home. Ice freezes
her being to frigid and brittle.
No fire to warm her, no flames to inspire

she bitterly winters
the cold.

Juliana Romnes

AMONG THE STARS

The sun will never understand the joy I experience,
as I bear witness to its arrival in the morning sky,
every day, right on schedule.

And the sun will never know the important role it plays,
when young plants grow tall,
by eating its light.

Yet, as it travels along its celestial route,
I often wonder if the sun is lonely.

94 million miles from the lives that it cultivated...
an eternal crackling fire, spinning in a void of darkness.

So, I wish I could tell the sun,
that there are more of its kind.
Millions of trillions, in fact.

And I wish I could tell the sun,
that it is among the stars,
and they know what it's going through.

And I wish the sun could feel my gratitude,
as I experience its warm, radiant glow,
before it merges with the horizon, to signal the end of the day.

And once the sun has set, its distant neighbors make
an appearance.
As I ponder life on their orbiting worlds, I drift to sleep,
until the next sunrise

Catherine Avery St. Jean

ST. JOHNS COUNTY LIBRARY SYSTEM

In St. Johns, where knowledge thrives,
A library system, our treasure lies.
Anastasia Island, a branch by the sea,
Whispers tales of adventure, wild and free.

Hastings Branch, a beacon of learning's light,
Welcomes young minds with warmth so bright.
Ponte Vedra Branch, where stories unfold,
Imagination takes flight, to wonders told.

Bartram Trail Branch, a haven so grand,
With books as companions, hand in hand.
Southeast Branch, where dreams find their way,
In every page turned, a new world to sway.

The Main Branch, a hub of knowledge and more,
With wisdom-filled shelves, a treasure trove in store.
Bookmobiles roam, bringing joy far and wide,
To every corner, they journey with pride.

As our community flourishes, leaps, and bounds,
We yearn for a new library or more, that astounds.
With eager anticipation, we await their embrace,
Spaces of discovery, expanding minds with grace.

So let our voices echo, with hope resound,
For the new libraries that will soon be found.
In St. Johns, our love for learning grows strong,
Bound by words, where we all will belong.

DeLand Boulevard Collective Poetry

Barbara Meistrell

AS THE SUN GOES DOWN

Smells of evening
as the sun goes down
coolness of dusk
settles on the ground

A hectic time
day almost done
evening shadows creep
bring a silence deep
when the sun goes down

The struggles of day
slowly, quietly fade away
those of night
awake
rest a moment
in the coolness
evening
makes
as the sun goes down

Little sounds barely heard
scurry on the ground
dogs bark
screen door bangs in the night
woman sits quiet
without light
makes no sound
as the sun goes down

36

Cigarette smoke weaves thru the air
glass of ice tinkles
makes woman aware
she sits quiet in the evening cool air
wondering
what in her day she missed
thoughts, feelings, images
of her life
go round and round
as the sun goes down

White Hat   by Jinny Kelley

Live Poets Society
of Daytona Beach

Marc Davidson

OR DON'T CHOOSE!

In Robert Frost's "Choose Something Like A Star"
the poet urges us to contemplate
the beauty that shines on us from afar
and what's behind that beauty. As if fate
could rest upon a ball of burning gas
a zillion miles away yet still somehow
exerting pull upon the human mass
and every tree, and ant, and fish, and cow.
It seems unlikely, yet much has been writ
of zodiac and fate that's in its sway
that governs human temperament and wit
and guides us, willy-nilly, in its way.
    A desperate state to find ourselves thus led
    with naught but starlight ruling in our head

Llewellyn McKernan

CORN HILL, TRURO, CAPE COD

Bending to the will
of the wind, the beach roses bury
their pink faces
in the sand, the slow wheel of the tide
goes by with its blue
and white spokes. No choking
that throttle. Every
piece of sun gets threaded.

The wind's electric
guitar starts up as dozens of dusty
millers* put out their
tongues, plowing the air
to no purpose. You and I
love, talking to
each other on Corn Hill,
lean into the wind,
our voices vanishing like
those going down
to the bottom
of a well.

How the foam
laughs when our feet get
near it—How the rim of the sky
grips the edge
of the sea, a blood-red
gown the ocean wears
as the sun, in an explosion
of scarlet, at last
is intent on setting.

*beach flowers.

41

Thomas McMahon OBS

THE OWL

huddled in a darkened tent
moon and midnight past
owl calls from shadowed woods
searching for its mate

soft hooting floats gently
splits the blackness of the night
carrying haunting messages
bridging silent slumbrous hours

a distant call answers
cloaked somewhere in the trees
unseen shadows whisper now
i drift into a dream

Ellen Nielsen

THE BRIDGE

We were called Alejandro, Carlos, Dorian,
Jose, Maynor, Miguel. We came here from
Mexico, Guatemala, Honduras, El Salvador.
We came alone, with our parents, with our wives,
with our children, to build new lives in *El Norte,*
in the glittering country of dreams. Instead,
we found hard work no one else would do.
We worked for a company that hired mostly
Latinos like us and didn't ask for a green card.
There was plenty of work, there were always
more cracks in the pavement, more potholes to fill.
We knew about the traffic, the danger, the drivers
who didn't slow down in construction zones,
the *pendejos* who threw their garbage at us.
That's why we were working so late at night
when most of them were asleep in their beds.
It was cold on the bridge so we wore work boots
and wool socks and hats and thick warm jackets.
In the water it would turn out not to matter.
We saw the ship coming down the channel.
It looked normal at first, then it went dark.
That's why it took too long to understand
that the ship was going to hit the bridge.
Some of us made it to our trucks, but too late
to drive off a bridge more than a mile long.
We heard a loud boom and the road tilted
and we slid into the river. We were trapped
in the black water under the cement truck
and jagged pieces of the bridge. It was so cold
it didn't take long to die, but we had time
to pray and say good-bye to our families.
Will anyone remember our names?

John Michael Sears

THE DELIGHTFULNESS OF THE ELUSIVE

long before there were charging kiosks for EVs,
before filling stations evolved to be self-service,
young men, such as myself, my hands rough and oily,
would check under the hood, clean the windshield,
while working weekends to pay my college fees –
but on days when Donna's Mustang would skid
to a stop beside our pumps, I'd have worked for free.

the most alluring debutante, once homecoming queen,
in her racing-striped, Playboy-pink graduation gift,
a '69 convertible, white-wall tires, white-vinyl seats,
but most of its sparkle just sat behind the wheel,
changing the radio stations, not bothering to speak –
until one afternoon during a drenching summer storm
after she'd driven two miles with the top down,
she gently pulls up to the pumps, shockingly forlorn,
even blinking twice while flipping wet blond curls,
pleading that I dry out her car before she dares take it home.

Donna knew she raced too many miles ahead of me,
her speeding pinkish blur too fast for me to ever catch,
but for years, while driving in the rain, I'd hope to see
that speeding pink convertible with its top down,
and Donna singing with the radio, a little wild, still carefree.

Kenneth Simon

EASTERN BLUEBIRD

A streak
blue line
cuts the near horizon,
glimmering
cerulean
fantasy.

A paintbrush
in an invisible hand
colors with
uncertain form.
True and gone.
Blink it away.

A phantom
coats the retina like the song
of a whisper
on the wind.
Stillness
is its color.

A rapture
for the eye
cleaves
imagination wide open
empty
waiting
to be filled.

Bruce Woodworth

HUMAN MUSIC ON A DUSTY EVENING

From the long-abandoned dry-cleaners,
now a temporary house of praise,
comes the raucous cry of witness.
This is the South, so there are snakes
and hallelujahs a-plenty.
Ragged souls cling to long-held conviction
that everyone is a sinner, praise Him,
and we are only built to suffer.

Down the block at the hardware,
three men sit on wooden stools sorting
nails that customers have dropped into
the wrong wooden kegs, uncaring beasts
that they are.
There are so many forms of sin about!

Talk ranges from who is starting for the Rays
to how bad the coffee is, and why Carl can't
get it right after all this time.
He can tune a carb, but the mechanics of
coffee still eludes him.

Carl grins. Salvation and perfection are for
those down the street. He can tell a brad
from a roofing nail without looking,
nicotine-stained fingers working their magic,
even as he deflects their jibes.

This wooden floor was here when they were
all born; may outlive them, in fact.
The only thing older is their faith, and all
the snakes in the world won't take the place
of an orderly keg of nails.

And the hallelujahs ring out as a drywall screw
bites Carl's stubby fingertip like a mishandled
serpent in a sinner's lying hands

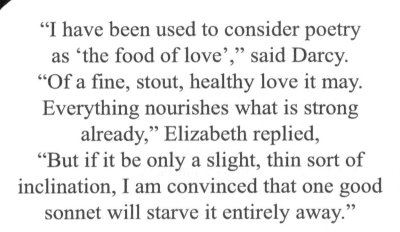

"I have been used to consider poetry
as 'the food of love'," said Darcy.
"Of a fine, stout, healthy love it may.
Everything nourishes what is strong
already," Elizabeth replied,
"But if it be only a slight, thin sort of
inclination, I am convinced that one good
sonnet will starve it entirely away."

Jane Austen, *Pride and Prejudice*

Miami Poets

Charles Maxim Bernstein

WHISPERED WORDS

The words we whisper
to each other when
we make love
are poems

unprintable,
unpublishable poems

They are rhythmic,
repetitive, recited
in sweet breathy lines
and passionate pauses

We won't be reading them
at open mic events

We aren't submitting
them to literary journals

They aren't getting in
this year's Florida anthology

Or next month's *Georgia Review*

Not even in the *très chic* pages
of the *Paris Review*

They are only for us

As necessary, as intimate,
as sensual . . .

. . . as the way we touch

Connie Goodman-Milone

Key deer
somehow survive
the storms

Marlene Kann

THE TEST

My friend asks,
"Are you still seeing
Your lover?
After all, it has been
Two years."
And I reply,
"Yes."
My friend asks,
"How do you manage
To keep the affair
Exciting? After all,
There are just so many
Items of lingerie, positions,
And whispered or grunted
Sweet nothings."
And I reply,
"Become the siren
Of seduction,
The sorceress of love.
Brew love's potion
And drink thirstily.
One's charms must
Rise above the ordinary."
I ask myself,
"Where would I be
Without you, my lover?"
And I reply,
"Sucked into the black
Hole of tedium."
Never.

Joanne Sherry Mitchell

SHE WAS A NUMBERS PERSON

Counting the tiles in the ceiling
The steps in each day
The number a heart beats a minute
What made the habit uninviting
She counted sorrows.

Each Saturday she spent the day
Checking each account
For balances, bills to be paid
Monies to be received.

When things went well
She counted sorrows
When things went poorly
She counted sorrows.

Gets up early
Goes to bed early
Plenty of time
For all her counting.

Ginger   by Jinny Kelley

New River Poets

Beverly A. Joyce

THE PATHWAY TO PROGRESS

It all began with the stone wheel,
Then came wagons and the automobile.
Now we have planes to soar the sky
To travel fast and travel high.

Once we corresponded by mail,
Our letters sent by horse and rail.
That time in history has flown,
Now we talk on the telephone.

Yesterday it was the typewriter,
Then invention's light shone brighter.
Now a computer does so much more
Than we could have ever hoped for.

Technology has closed many gaps
With inventions, programs, and apps,
But it can never, ever replace
The creative, superior human race.

Janet Watson

FLIGHT PLAN TO YUCATAN

This tiniest of birds,
having spent a summer
sipping the nectar
of northern gardens and fields,
now perches in October dusk
on a Gulf Coast mangrove twig.
The hummingbird's slender bill
points westward,
across water that reflects
fading ribbons of sunset.
A seasonal wisdom
beckons him to fly alone
to where the sun has disappeared–
a place he's never seen.

To complete the pilgrimage
that his mother made
several times before his birth,
he will carry a light payload
of delicate bones
and a rapidly-beating heart
the size of an apple seed.
He will fly by the map in his head
through all the coming darkness
and tomorrow's light,
only inches above the waves,
until the sea's breath
carries the scent of land.
His wings will hum him
into tropical forest,
where the open throats
of flowers have waited for him.

Betty Ann Whitney

ABOUT LIVING

I am grateful –
for this morning, for your bright smile,
for the slow conversation
between you and me, about nothing really,
but meaningful to us after last night's
medical rescue, your heart racing,
your heavy gasps hungering breath.

Yes – grateful to be here at your bedside,
your nurse unaware of my help
with your sipping cool water through a straw.
I want to care for you – want
to comb your hair, smooth lotion
over your scars, feel your hand in mine,
our promise of unbroken love
all these sixty-two years.

I am thankful for the beauty grown inside us,
from two people, not yet twenty – happy
to be filled with each other, your faith in us
strengthening mine, your strong-armed hugs
and warm kind hands, a blessing as
we blossomed, like meadows of summer sun.

I am especially grateful for today,
together, comfortably relaxed
in the legacy of us.

Some things remain simple, like,
your puckered lips as you lean in close,
the clue you have always given
for me to receive the certainty of forever
with your gentle kiss.

We do not know yet that by sundown,
I will be your widow.

Blue Springs Ibis   by Daniel Stone

North Florida
Poetry Hub

Suzanne S. Austin-Hill

FLORIDIAN CLIMATIC CONTRASTS

Summer heat like a wild fire,
challenged by single threads of sweat -
  between breasts,
  tracing the spine.

Fall indistinct in character,
evasive in commitment;
  feigning loyalty,
  a tree mocks deciduousness.

Winter temperatures' plummet force a brisk gait;
faux allegiance to the cardinal
  hop-scotching on lifeless branches
  wrapped in frozen tears.

Spring whispers a warm, dehumidifying call
causing buds to respond from somewhat naked boughs;
  worn and torn by prior, erratic,
  irreverent atmospheric conditions, it persists.

Kenneth Boyd

ISABEL

...divided between our worlds, waiting partly blind
Hushed I say your name—Isabel—God's promise
Witness of your prescient marble unfurling

With firstborn billows, day of birth now recurring
Your curtained appeasement, your motionless solace
Veiled docent reigning, finessing your chiseled shrine

Renewing the virtue of your breath of softness
Opaque wrinkles of the stars' drape of vested times
Did you want more? Is your promise what you nurture?

Shout your unfurling promise to the waiting blind

Based on *Isabel II Veiled* by Camillo Torregiano (1855)

63

Sally Wahl Constain

UP IN THE AIR

What determines our fate?
Maybe there are some mischievous
merrymakers up somewhere,
partying and playing games
with our happiness.
Tossing coins, rolling dice,
jumping for joy when
the roulette wheel
runs a foul.

I want my money back. I want
a try at one more game of chance.
Just one more time, before
the casino shuts its door.

Shutta Crum

THE OLD TRAVELER FINDS ME

This wind—the oldest of travelers—
rushes through an open door and puts his feet up.
Disheveled, weary. Yet, he bears gifts.

From a room high above the city of Florence
where sheer curtains rise and drift like music,
you stand in the heat, draped only in a white sheet.
We gaze out the window—another feature
of the Boboli Gardens.

From a Mexican beach where the starlight
rides each small tongue of water.
You, your toes in the wind-whipped foam
listening to the dark while I linger,
beguiled by the taste of salt.

From a northern forest deep in winter,
the air heavy with the scent of pine.
And you, lifting my face toward yours,
while ghost-like dancers rise ensorcelled
from the snow to whirl about us.

All this, from a door I left open
and an old traveler come to make himself at home.

Laura Dill

SHATTERED TIME

It loiters now, casually propped
against the damp basement wall,
its cames bowed and panes
punctured by some random ball;
a game of catch gone wrong.

Paint, weathered and chipped,
the red-braced cross and gothic peaks,
a reminder it graced a chapel once,
misty green and gold shimmering down,
dappling prayerful faces lining pews
where small bottoms squirmed, and
white-gloved mommas shushed.

Chris Kastle

nibbling the shoreline
watery teeth
always hungry

Previously published in *Cold Moon Journal*, July 2, 2024

Mary McAllister

PERSPECTIVE

Nobody would think it unusual
To lie on the floor of the A train
In New York City.

There are no conductors to
Tell you to get up
No subway guards to move you along

You have only yourself and the vibrations
Of the wheels on steel and
Your thoughts rumbling all the way down

If you're a city girl it might be
The way you get in touch with a different kind of nature
It's just a train; you get on or you don't.

Beth Ramos

THE CRAYON BOX

I couldn't find the black to show my soul
so I pulled out the blues.

They felt warm
and I felt odd because
blue is cool, according to the books.

The rhythm of the sort captured me.
I was amazed at the range
between peach and magenta,
and that blood red landed with
sepia and asparagus rooted in the corner,
                                        right.

The neons, yellows mostly,
are left back,
(so I won't be startled by their brightness.)

Thistle and timber wolf surround the blues,
now center front.

I know the black *is*
in there, somewhere,
but it's unimportant now.
After all, it *is*
only one of ninety-six
colors in the crayon box.

Royal Palm Literary Award for Poetry Second Place – 2008

Sipra Roy

SPIRIT-IN-SILENCE.

What can be more eloquent than *silence*
in the vessel of any language?
However delicate or complicated,
    Language is designed merely
    An external apparel or costume of feeling!
    Feeling is too subtle to be exposed
    In any vehicle of language.
    More the feeling goes profound,
    More the speech looses its sound,
    Becomes dumb but Super-sensitive!
    Like the primitive one of by-gone-days.
    Love, hate, jealousy, or fear
    All suppressed, hidden, unspoken words
    Reflect messages either in eyes
    Or in body gesture
    Just as do the innocent animals!
    In the vessel of language
    Nothing is more eloquent
    Than the Spirit-in-Silence!

Sharon Scholl

PHOTO ALBUM: SENIOR PROM

The almost-man in a rented suit pretends
to look casual, as if, like Fred Astaire,
he was born to tux and tails.

His unruly thatch of hair is newly subdued
by the family barber. His smile flickers
between shy and boy-devilish.

The corsage his mother chose lies trembling
on the shoulder of a nubile date whose father snaps
the photo while flashing a protective frown.

Suave is what he's aiming for with a jingle
of car keys, that pretense of independence.
He mentally reviews memorized etiquette,
the expectations of these refinements.

The photo has a rosy cast betraying age,
time's accumulation now so thick
the grown man scarcely sees himself
in this mirror of his youth. Only now
he weeps for how beautiful it was.

Ruth Van Alstine

TEARS FOR DADDY

Sitting in my father's house
it's quiet now, almost always is.
As we two exist together,
enmeshed in a tangled dance
that began suddenly, just months ago.

Before Mom died, it was different.

She would be here in her recliner,
talking, moving, moaning, groaning,
playing books on tape obnoxiously loud,
taking her anger and despair
of declining health and vision
out on all of us, but mostly Daddy,
to vent her pain.

Yet he stayed strong for her out of love,
never complaining, always patient.

She died so suddenly,
no time for him to say goodbye.
In grieving for his wife
his body collapsed and stroked,
only wanting to join his bride.

But God had other plans.

She is here, I know it.
She left flowers for Daddy on the doorstep
the other day, to say she was sorry.

Now I care for my father,

body broken,
and spirit for living.

It's quiet here now, almost always is.
So different from before, and yet so much the same.
Sometimes I look out the window,
watch the trees,

and cry.

Previously published *Shattered Moonbeams*, 2016

"Poetry is a deal of
joy and pain and
wonder, with a dash
of the dictionary."

Kahlil Gibran

Northwest Florida Poets

Mary Gutierrez

LOOK HOMEWARD ANGEL

The raven waits patiently, keeping time,
as the sunset's crimson skies embrace another day's end.
We wait, sharing sacred stories of long ago,
of a time filled with hope and happiness,
of a time scarred with secrets and lies.
A raw realization drowns us,
the flow that has passed will never pass again.

Nearby, the clock chimes mockingly,
reminding us of things to come
while the intoxicating smell of blooming hyacinths
burst in through open windows,
stealing space in a sunless room.

We are paralyzed by this moment,
yet we still wait, saying too much, not saying enough.
We carry the wounds of a life lived too deeply,
making the transition heavy with sadness and sorrow,
and causing our hearts to break under the pressure.

The mirrors are now covered and
the clock chimes no more.
A blackness unifies us as our individuality
has morphed into collective grief.

Yet far beyond this place,
candles flicker in expectation,
from death to morning,
lighting the path for weary travelers.

Look homeward Angel,

you can go home again.

This piece was previously published in the anthology, *Words in a Web,* 2023.

Claire Massey

EIGHT WAYS TO LOOK AT COMPUTER KEYBOARDS

1. All the world's centuries
of hieroglyphics
compressed into two handfuls
of symbols

2. Portal to the dawn
of enlightenment
or a long night of lies

3. Voice for the voiceless denied
the power of physical speech

4. Smorgasbord of choices
to shift beliefs:
control, enter, insert, delete

5. A winged Mercury delivering
lonely-heart profiles,
an intermediary for courting
illusory Venuses

6. The means of avoiding
person-to-person,
the body language that betrays
emotion
Underlines, all caps,
bold, shouting fonts
offer the cowardly
an easy way out

7. Everyone's AI therapist
dispensing 24/7
generic prescriptions for heartache

8. The ultimate planchette
whizzing 'round the planet's
Ouija board
propelled by eight billion fingertips.

Carolyn Joyce Tokson

OLD MAN CYPRESS

What memories dwell in the branches of the Old Man Cypress?
What remembrances linger in the roots
sending up knees and buttresses,
shallow roots spreading over twenty feet
before they reach down
into Mother Earth?

With an easy life span of 600 years
he was here on this river
before the first Spaniards gave it
the name "Perdido."
The Pensacola, Muscogee, Choctaw, and Creek
tribes lived along her shores
fishing, hunting game
long before the explorers under Tristan de Luna y Arellano.
Many years later, the cartographer gave her
the Rio Perdido name "Lost," hidden in the palmetto,
longleaf pine, and cypress.

Barren now of the long branches of needles
bright green in spring,
orange in the winter,
he stands naked.
How many generations of eagles and hawks
have nested in the Old Man's branches
which bent in the wind and then stood upright?
How many smaller birds and squirrels have
survived on the tiny cones falling in the breezes?
How many catfish nest in hollow trunks nearby?

But the Old Man Cypress stands silent.
His stories are known only to the stars,
the clouds, the rain. Perhaps he speaks
to an eagle resting on his journey. Or to the moon.
Or to the roots of other trees.
Still, we cannot hear. His story is not for our ears.
It is a language too old for us,
lost like the river once was.

Andrea Jones Walker

LISTENING TO JIMMY BUFFET IN WALMART

Blue skies, yellow leaves,
autumn breeze
I'm shopping at Walmart on a carefree day
when the voice of a wistful Jimmy Buffet
comes over the pipes,
brings notes of nostalgia and melancholy.
Come Monday,
nothing can be returned.

Lori Zavada

AFTER THANKSGIVING

The driveway is empty, the house quiet.
Three leaves hang on the redbud tree,
sure to be gone by nightfall.

Hot tea soothes my gluttonous hangover,
fused with licorice, vanilla, and mint.
Fennel's sweet finish is a ceremony.

Christmas lights twinkle in oak-fingered woods,
distant cars swoosh by on their way to shops,
and I struggle to absorb absence,

coats piling up on the guest room bed,
refrigerator and stovetop overflowing,
Alexa playing something we all agree on,

the bread ring I make once a year,
vegan sweets my stepdaughter bakes,
ice cream for e-v-e-r-y-t-h-i-n-g,

deviled eggs my stepson has mastered,
the random hot-peppered one
that earns bragging rights for a year,

the slide show my husband sets to music,
whiteboard for charades,
old Cool Whip containers we fill with leftovers.

Laughter vibrates the windows,
and makes the bricks bulge,
before fading with the winter sunset.

One by one
they leave.
We say *so long for now*

entrust our jokes,
memories, and gratitude,
to each other for safekeeping.

I steep another tea bag,
pretending to appreciate the silence,
and count the days until our next feast.

Fairy Door

by Elaine Person

Orlando Area Poets

Fred Briggs

HOME OFFICE

The papers,
scattered on the floor.
   Too painful to straighten up.
They say someone is gone.

No notice,
just up and out
  with the pictures and the order.
  And the papers scattered.

Little left.
Just what used to be,
packed into boxes and stacked.
   Ready to throw away.

This room,
so messy and empty.
   My heart, so empty and messy,
and no one to straighten up.

Teresa TL Bruce

BODY WORKS

I've clearly lost my mind, what with my
head up in the clouds. It's not on straight
at all, and I'm in way over my own head this high
and likely soon to fall if I don't get a grip—too late!

While spinning down head over heels,
I got off on the wrong foot, so now it feels
my gait's askew. (I really don't know what to do.)

Since I'm all ears, with all myself to the ground,
will I stumble and trip, spreading ears all around?
In nobody's business, I lost my nose,
cut off despite my face,
and since the cat has got my tongue
I've lost both sense of smell and taste.

My stiff upper lip won't let smiles come free,
and I think somebody's got their eyes on me.
I'm kind of freaking out back there,
on the back of my head, where I feel their stare.
(No wonder I'm pulling out my hair.)

I'm trying not to writhe or twitch,
but it hurts not to scratch a seven-year itch.
My bio-clock wintered, fell, and sprung.
I'm far too old to feel half so un-young.

And I don't mean to gripe or whine,
but has anybody by chance, maybe, perhaps
seen my missing spine?
I don't know how to weather this lapse

Lela E. Buis

A PHONE LINE TO HEAVEN

Why isn't there a phone line to heaven?
There are people I need to talk to,
to ask for advice and support
when life goes wrong somehow.

Mom, I need to tell you your cat died,
the one I took over when you passed away
two years ago, the sweet calico…
She was all I had left of you,

And Dad, I need to talk to you
about growing old and how to deal
with all the ins and outs of infirmity
that you handled so well.

And dear heart, I need to tell you I love you.
I thought you would always be there for me.
I need to hear your voice on the phone
just one more time.

—In Memorium: Rodney Gordon Crittenden (1946–2023)

Gary Childress

surf's up, grab your board
I'm sorry for everything
a dying swan sings

Chris Flocken

THE RICH REWARDS OF
AN INVESTMENT IN BIRDSEED

A commotion of songbirds swooping, sauntering,
hopping, hovering, fluttering, flickering, flitting, and flirting,
filling the air with their cacophonous song:
tweeting, twittering, trilling, chittering, chattering,
cooing, cawing, chirping, and whistling.

An octet of cardinals sharing a perch at the bird feeder
take flight in unison when spooked by a curious dog nearby.
As they arise, they display a smorgasbord of reds from tawny
tans to russet reds to the radiant splendor of scarlet.

A bird of luminescent blue darts from
the cover of the Eastern Red Cypress,
soars across the grass, into the welcoming
arms of a privet hedge.

The Southern Red Maple, once again in full leaf, is refuge
and respite to a cosmopolitan abundance of songbirds:
sparrows, robins, bluejays, mockingbirds, chickadees,
swallows, goldfinches, indigo buntings, wrens, and
yellow-rumped warblers.

Even the woodpeckers, mourning doves, starlings,
and crows contribute to the symphony of the season.
After a long, dreary winter, springtime in the North Carolina
Piedmont is a verdant botanical and ornithological delight.

Peter M. Gordon

ANTIQUING IN ALLEN, MICHIGAN

After four hours marching through miles
of Antique Malls, our expedition feels more
like endurance test than treasure hunt.

Seasoned searchers carry water bottles, beef
jerky, granola. They knew musty malls on this
strip of State Road Twelve don't sell food.

Our lust for cheap relics to flip for a fortune
overcomes hunger, pushes us to parade past booth
after booth crammed with past lives' possessions.

We pass crates filled with vinyl records preserved
in plastic bags, and I puzzle why so many people
bought Mantovani and Perry Como. We unearth

treasures from our youth – Nehru jackets, Flintstone other
family sets of glassware, Beatles board games, subway maps,
our delight not shared by children who glue eyes to phones.

When we falter, experienced hunters assure us these
multitudes of oak and maple dressers, rocking chairs,
Depression glass, *Life, Look*, magazines are only a warmup

for Hog Creek Antiques, double the size of any mall.
But now my feet ache, back's sore, and worse, children
complain these talismans from our youth are only musty junk.

If there is treasure here, why are so many selling?
In the sixties I poked holes in baseball cards to hew
to bicycle spokes, pretended flipping sounds were

motorcycles revving. In Allen these pasteboard pictures
sell ten dollars each. We make a momentous decision
to skip Hog Creek. Drive back to Marshall for ice cream;

cold sweet vanilla and butter pecan in waffle cones
restore our souls. I don't want them to remember
furniture. I want them to remember love.

Angela Griner

TRAIL MAINTENANCE

I walked for a few miles
   carrying a heavy load
   of things I could not understand.

With each step, left then right, then left again
   the load began to shift and turn
   and show itself, piece by piece,
   one by one, each unmarked stone.

Eventually, I started to give each one a name.
Eventually, I could lay this one down here in this way
   and another one here just so,
   creating little altars
   every couple of steps.

What had been weighing me down
   and laying me out
   began to mark my way,
   trail markers for the way back home.

Carlton Johnson

A DIP

The pool guys are dressed in hoodies today
59 degrees is a bit nippy. Anyone for a dip?

I muse over my blueberries and muesli.
Everything is above the surface. Now,

I ponder getting dressed, walking to the car.
It isn't far. Sometimes my legs don't follow

as if the stream of life is pulling me forward, my feet
want to stop and enjoy the scenery or lurch

forward while my top half tries to avoid
the jetties of counter, desk, doorjamb.

They are still there with their skimmers cleaning
while I stare at the eddies in my coffee, treading water.

Denis Keeran

A MAN

What is it makes a man A Man?
A question sometimes pondered.
Is it prowess on the playing field?
Or with his buddies bonded?

Is it suaveness with the ladies?
A style that makes them swoon?
These traits, and others, may be true
But not with these alone.

A Man is always gentle, available with thought.
But stands his ground with firmness,
to ease those ones distraught.
When making hard decisions, with kindness does consult.
And weighing all his options, compassion will result.

A Man is gen'rous, therefore blessed,
And shares his time and gold.
He's sensitive to different views,
And never harsh or cold.

He stoops to meet a child's own eye,
And bathes them with his smiles.
With Nature's fold to benefit,
He'll join their walk for miles.

I'm sure there's more words can be writ,
And stories more be told.
To be A Man requires much…
A Treasure to behold!

Wicker and Key Lime Pie   by Emily Sujka

Judith Kovisars

A LOVE SONG SUNG

Under the limbs of the spreading live oak
That was here before I was an idea–
Lit not by the moon,
But by antique lanterns,
Golden, that stood in a noble place
Somewhere and time I do not know.

With the sound of the cicada
Stringing endless urgency
Of a summer's night song,
I hear the laughter of children
Playing in the leaves.

This is my secret garden
Within a time that is outside time
And in a place that is in time but nowhere.

It is the suicide point for those
Who have not chanced the leap of faith
Into their souls.
This is where I am most alive in my self
And where your reality for me is clear.

I drink wine that is too warm for enjoyment
Tasting the heavy fruit bouquet,
Within a night that enshrouds in blue black velvet
I see the silver snail's trace upon the stones.

You are the still point of my soul,
The rose petals not yet open to the sun,
The perfect note played once upon a violin,
A silver kite loosed from its string
Soaring freely upon lightning-lined clouds,
An alpha and omega beyond the discovery
Of pi squared and the apple's falling.

What I am, I am, and you are what you are,
Simple as the beetles crawling and the spider's web,
The turning and returning
Back to the beginning and the ending.

To the place that is no place,
To the time outside of time,
To the pure white light that illuminates
And throws no shadow.

The still point in the garden
Of breathless laughter without sound,
Of a glimpse through the cracked stone wall
Covered with tiny blood red roses.

Nancy K. Hauptle MacInnis

STOMPIN' AT THE SAVOY*

Getting' ready for some Stompin' At The Savoy— Boy! So grab your finest suit coat, I'll slip on my peach and white fringe flapper, we will be the caper couple, no stubble now, trim those eyebrows, I'll tame my wild flaxen mane, put on your patent leathers, your finest pair of spitz and we'll tip the world on its jazzy axis, remake an aura of evening lights the likes of no aurora borealis. Oh yes— London Town, Paris, New York, get ready for this grand pair from Central Florida, an eclipse so fair, a glimpse of tropical fancy Gatsby all sharp and serene on the green, tailored, two-stepping, arresting eyes of dance-lovers everywhere— Without hesitation we'll slide a Tango, we'll Charleston, and Swing, we'll Samba sway to take heartbeats away— racing just trying to trace the steps of class and panache, and afterwards, when the sounds of supple songs and laughter subside, come take a rest on The Garden Terrace among fans of palm-frond umbrellas, sip an aperitif, whiff a bit of snuff for the nose, or take a puff of tobacco, just bask in all the joy— Stompin' At The Savoy.

*(Song by Benny Goodman)

.

102

"What can be explained is not poetry.
It is when the powers of explanation desert him
that the poet writes verse."

John Butler Yeats

Writing to his son, poet W.B. Yeats

Holly Mandelkern

OVERTURES ON VALENTINE'S DAY

In London's Covent Garden,
a young man is sidewalk-singing for pennies.
A passerby in a stylish fur-lined jacket and cap
joins him in "All I Ask of You" from *Phantom.*
He can't believe this stunning singer is standing here.
He wipes his brow and asks her,
"Do I... carry on?"

He carries on, her voice soaring with his,
his natural tenor matching her mezzo.
I wonder if he knows she's the lead singer
in *Phantom* at Her Majesty's Theatre.

For four minutes they're in love in front of strangers.
Overdressed, he throws down his woolen scarf
wanting no barrier, living
in the heat of the moment.
Crossing his arms over a bursting heart,
radiant and holding back tears,
he embraces being in the middle
of this memory, his eyes saying,
"Can you believe this is happening?"

A few shoppers pause to listen to this magic.
She leans toward him, touching his shoulder
as they pass the microphone between them.
As the song is ending, she points to pounds
a few onlookers toss his way, but he waits
for his turn and for her eyes on his
when they sing together.

He stands in this moment, not noticing the coins,
amazed at the coincidence of her presence.
Perhaps tomorrow he'll believe
she wasn't a phantom but his lucky penny
with a chance to be more
than a sidewalk show.

Beachy Keen   by Elaine Person

Mary Marcelle

BLOOM

I've beaten you about your trunk
with a shovel handle, like the
old nurseryman taught me to do,
grunting to get what I want.

You're scabbed with lichen
and craving the sweet coquina from
the now-paved road
that dusted lime at your roots.

But a week later
I take a deep breath of
the lemon-velvet air of February.

Fireworks.

Frank T Masi

IT STRIKES A CHORD

It strikes a chord...
when I see high school students board a bus
from a long waiting line.
It was an innocent era
when laughter and friendships were all that mattered
though I was standing on the edge of time.

It strikes a chord...
when I hear a baby cry–
still mystified by this act of creation.
It thrills me to this day–
a gift that fires my faith
and a constant source of elation.

It strikes a chord...
when I attend a wedding
and thrill to the organ's tune.
Bride and groom share the music
that will bind them forever,
but their future will come too soon.

It strikes a chord...
when I enter a church...
and remember my calling–
to be of service to those in need
to keep the faith
to ride out the storm
when dark skies are falling.

The striking of a chord…
resonates the music of life.
It's a lyrical concert hall
with a permanent seat
though you only attend occasionally
but whose music you will always recall.

Caryn McCleskey

I AM WORDS

I am words, sentences, paragraphs
compressed into my sinews,
paper scraps stashed among
the pleats of my life.

I am diamond-hard syllables
that tumble streaming from my pen,
a pebble-slide from brain to fingertips.

A letter cavalcade no longer flanked
by oppression, coercion, embrace,
leads me out of childhood's confusion, love's labyrinth,
the maze of malignant married manipulations of memories
and moods.

I write as rescue, creation, declaration
of independence, existence, selfhood
no longer erased, scratched out, deleted,
but inked, printed **Arial Bold** and true.

Diane Neff

THE END OF WAR

The rutted paths worn bare by soldiers' boots
have faded, smoothed from years of wind and rain
with grasses grown tall over rough terrain
and dandelions sending down their roots.
The sacrifices made in war reduced
to memories, decisions made in pain
and not forgotten, pulse throughout every vein
as strong as rising sap in northern spruce.
And when the last of warriors will have gone
to their rewards, escaping private hell
where keeping silent, never to defend
their actions, finally come to brightening dawn,
the sun shines gold, a gentle, warm farewell,
and soothes the dreamers, lets the nightmares end.

This poem was published in *Proud to Be: Writing by American Warriors, Volume 11 (2022)* published by the Missouri Humanities & Southeast Missouri State University Press

Elaine Person

LET THE LIGHT IN

The night was dark. Sue sat all alone.
No one called her on the phone.
With lights off, she isolated
into another night she hated.

Then an idea hit her head:
"I'll open up to the world instead."
She cracked the window, opened the door.
"I don't have to be alone anymore."

She let the light in through the crack,
opened up to never go back.
If it's camaraderie you lack,
step outside and let the light in
and let the adventure begin.

You won't know unless you grow.
Let your inner sparkle show.
Look toward the light; you'll be all right.
Open up and then take flight.

She walked down the street in her lovely town
and saw happy people all around
She felt great without making a sound.
She stepped outside and let the light in
and let the adventure begin.

Soon a friendly man approached her.
He smiled, and Sue's subconscious coached her.
"Hi, I'm Sue." "I'm John," he replied,
"do you want to go for coffee?" Sue felt happy inside.

She only had to open her door a crack.
Now her life will never lack.
John and Sue did more than snack.
They stepped outside and let the light in.
They let their adventure begin.

Together, their heads are in a spin.
You can see their happy grins.
Open the door and everyone wins.
Step outside and let the light in.
Let your adventure begin.

Lynn Schiffhorst

LA VIE EXISTAIT

Le soleil pur, le nom doux du petit village,
Les belles oies qui sont blanches comme le sel...
Se mêlent a mon amour d'autrefois
Francis Jammes (1868–1938)

Something in me was not reborn,
but stays there, back there,
there where . . .
I let my mind wake up
and stretch itself under an unhurried sun.

I stroll to town through an avenue of oak trees
while mist burns off from the fields beyond them.
I join my slow, unhurried neighbors
who open their grandfathers' shops
after going to Mass at dawn on weekdays.

In an office flavored with sun-warmed ink
and heavy with oaken desks,
I write out wills and deeds and contracts.
Great changes are born from my right hand.

I eat my *déjeuner* at Chez Suzanne,
which takes its name from the church
with its stained glass window
showing Susanna shaming the elders.

At night in the parlors of farmers,
whose business letters my father wrote,
I drink a few glasses of home-made marc,
and listen to old, old men and women
telling their older stories,

all of them dressers of sycamores
and bakers of hearth cakes.

Part of me, the larger, greater
part of me, is there.
I comfort the part that isn't
by remembering these five things,

"The trees you walk under now
grew up from the ancient, original trees,
roads are essentially ageless,
no engineer can hurry the sun,
old men and women still hold fast
to wisdom they want to deposit
in welcoming soil,

and God, Who dwelled in the old dim churches,
is waiting here still
to lift you up on the pure gold paten
of His timelessness."

Title translation: *Life Existed*
Translation from Francis Jammes:
The pure sun, the sweet name of the little village,
the beautiful geese that are as white as salt. . .
mingle with my love of the old days.

déjeuner (line 20): *lunch*
line 29, *Dressers of sycamores, Amos 7:14*
line 30, *Bakers of hearth cakes, 1 Kings 19:6*

Carolynn J. Scully

WEDDING WINE

A mother's plea,
and Father's permission,
introduced the mission
for the Son destined
to be the true vine.

Wedding feast joy
turned sour
with guests'
empty cups.
Time arrived for a sign
of life's celebration.

Water, a life source,
became seed planted
into earthen jars.
The fruit of the Spirit
grew and was pressed
into drink created
through His word.

The best wine
was saved till last.

Shelley Stocksdale

PEACEMAKER
PRESIDENT
CARTER

President Carter bridged ties
to the People's Republic of China,
started SALT II, for fewer nukes,
with Brezhnev's Soviet Union;
gave up our U.S. control
over their Panama Canal,
wrestled Middle East peace
between Egypt and Israel, then
signed Camp David Accord. Here on
home field, he harvested yields in energy,
education and our endangered environment.

Through his and helpmate Rosalynn's
wonderful, caring Carter Center:
    Addressing public policy,
    nationally and internationally,
    staff and associates join President
    Carter *to resolve conflict, promote
    democracy, protect human rights,
    prevent disease and other afflictions.*

Carter won his Nobel Peace Prize
for brave diplomacy and sublime
worldwide mankind triumph.

Emily M. Sujka

OUT INTO MY WORLD

With music still ringing in my ears,
The winds try to steal me
Get a grip on whipping blonde reins
Yanking my hair
and me
Out of the car window,
Headfirst.
Where is there to go,
But out into the world
Where the heart roams uncaged
The soul goes off course.
It's not whose world,
What world,
Which world,
There are no questions.
My world
The one that I
And my suitcase
Land on.
The one that
My feet and my being
Add tread to.
The one that
My lungs inhale
As I roll up the glass
And my head settles in.
With each altimeter
The music further quiets
Distance from the memory,
Mountainous ear plugs.

Alpine heights' snares
Gradually slacken—
Let go.
It hadn't caught a being like it thought,
Humming in retreat
No need
As I'm already my own wind.

Jenni Sujka

BETRAYAL

Didn't think I would experience betrayal at 31
When life is only beginning.
I was supposed to have more time
Before the aches and pain begin.
Muscle disappearing and pain,
Never-ending doctors' appointments.
Youth, away with one diagnosis.
Mind, slowly crawling away like an attacked victim begging,
The question: Is this what death feels like?

Stan K. Sujka

POMEGRANATE
Dedicated to love and Granada, Spain

Mystical beauty
A flower mesmerizes
as hypnotist's watch
Exploding color of love

You are
The forbidden fruit
A womb like flower
With a secret moist and sweet
A gift from God

A fruit to be opened slowly,
Carefully, gently, tenderly
Stripping the shell
Revealing the nakedness

I lick your lips of scarlet
Taste the richness of your seed
Heaven in my mouth
I babble with joy

With a proper crown
You are my queen
Filled with 613 mitzvot of the Torah
Fruit, fertility, and
love.

Mark Andrew James Terry

ABOUT ACCOLADES
Philippine Sonnet

Most never hear a golden buzzer sound
or feel the thrill applause and cheers resound.
They'll never wield the power being crowned—
by royal name renowned from all-around.

Most won't be chosen for the Nobel Prize,
or write the lines that students memorize.
They won't have lived a life to novelize,
or soar in private jets across the skies.

But just perhaps that crown, those accolades,
are like the pythons in the everglades—
who hunt and slither through the muhly blades,
a feral snake no native prey evades.

Awards are feral too, though well-deserved,
by overwhelming others who have served.

Written for FSPA's 2024 Cadence Anthology

Cheryl Lynn West

TWO CHAIRS

No, you may not sit in that chair,
the empty one in the garden.
Do not move it.
Let it remain unoccupied.
It was his.
Together we sat,
he in his chair,
I in mine,
separated by a table
which held our morning coffee.
Take another seat
across the patio,
away from me.
I choose this spot,
where I will stay.
Two chairs.
One cup.

Shari Yudenfreund-Sujka

DECEPTION

It starts out with a little fib,
And works its way around,
Until it twists and turns enough,
So that the truth can not be found.
It winds it way around the facts,
'Til now it is a lie,
To try and hide its evil ways,
That will never die.
The truth has now been cloaked in
Falsehoods,
The deception is now complete,
For now we have been sold a bill of goods,
To make the matter a *fait accompli*.

Poetry For the Love Of It

Regardless   by Suzanne Austin-Hill

Charles Hazelip

CREATIVITY

Creativity, like a scented candle
Drifts aromas to find souls to handle
Thoughtful changes in customary ways
Altering longtime norms of routine days.

Like talking to oneself in whispered tones,
Creativity scurries by woeful moans
To find, somewhere in a hurrying mind,
A new uplifting glimpse of better times.

It could be a hike down a natural trail,
Or starting to create something with nails,
Or cleverly planting lovely flower beds,
Or improving how poor children are fed.

Wafting scents of this candle's sweet fuse
Can even guide poets ever seeking their muse.

Dorothy Kamm

TREES

That which gives the most
      Beauty

Is also the most deadly
      When a whirl of high wind
Snakes its way through

Tree canopies, branches curving
      Towards one another,
Touching but not embracing

Without the support of one another
      In the tornadic storm
          Cracked,
      And by their own sheer weight
Crashed down

Old growth gone
In a brief moment.

Louise Pare-Lobinsky

THE COSMIC DANCE

"May I have this dance?" said the Moon.

"Why, yes," said the Sun.
"I knew you would come."

The Sun shone in her orange golden splendor
As she twirled behind her partner,
Letting his dark suit and tails
Obscure her beauty
For the duration of the dance.

"But I have to let myself be seen a *little* bit," she said
                                        with a coy wink.
The Moon replied, "My love, I would not have it otherwise."

And so he only obscured her completely for a small path.
Many viewing their dance saw them both.

At long last, sadly, the dancing had to end.
The Moon released his partner,
who resumed her glorious place
in the shining afternoon sky.
The people viewing them were utterly transformed,
some vowing they would see the dance again.

It was,
indeed,
a magnificent dance.

Diane Colvin Reitz

SOUTHERN WRITERS

Southern writers
write about what
they wipe on their
sleeves, then lie
about it on paper.

They witness,
they observe,
they get everything
they deserve.

Their greatness lies
in their addictions
to the underbelly.
Revealing truth.

Tell an old southern joke
to some old southern folk.
Sounds funny until
the end, then drops flat

to the bottom of the page.

Gary J. Weston

CHERISHED CHRISTMAS

When I was a child, Christmas morning was so bright
I'd jump for joy out of my bed at the dawn's first light
Then tiptoe to my parents room or to the Christmas tree
To see what presents might be found, with a good degree of glee

In later years, with children, the glee remained but changed
As toys were found, were bought, were wrapped,
                                  and finally arranged
I was not quite as happy then to sleep a shorter night
But rose on Christmas morning hoping Santa got it right

And then there were some grandkids, to carry on tradition
To gather around the Christmas tree, or cookies in the kitchen
December 25th for them was also filled with joy
When they'd check very early for a hoped-for favorite toy

Christmas is more quiet now, with calls and cards and Zoom
It is no longer practical to gather in one room
But we cherish all the Christmases we've had along the way
And feel so very fortunate for this family holiday

Linda Whitefeather

ONE DAY INTO NIGHT

I am like butter
Melting in my chair
A mellow yellow
In cool flowing air

The sun is shining
Blinds are aflutter
Against window glass
I am like butter

As the day wears on
My eyes simply stare
I sit in dim light
Melting in my chair

The night sky grumbles
It's no longer mellow
But my lamplight is
A mellow yellow

Watching TV shows
From my comfy chair
While rain falls gently
In cool flowing air

Space Coast Poets

C. Cory Craig

HIS FATHER TAUGHT HIM THE RULES OF THE ROAD

Just drive she said
And they raced
night falling like a shroud
Those people are crazy she said
They drive me crazy

He went north
The south held only water
the music carried on it
He needed road to drive
On the map he
headed straight up
beyond Canada to sky
He passed lands
pink and green and yellow
the rivers curling an
impossible blue

She threw her head back
bared her teeth to
wind blowing through
eyes streaming
Faster she said

He would never stop
Guns to glass
pressed to an ear
Fear circling in
packs of sepia stone
arches in years in
empty apartments in
languages learned
on TV Faster
He did not tell her
he could love her

                                        Those words in our
                                        new slang so stiff
                                        He did not speak
                                        of life before this
                                    When he was still young
                                        and still

They're going to kill us all
These words came from
behind her hand
and her eyes went soft
He touched her breast
her hair
She leaned into his palm
his fingers in her hair
69 is sexy she said
It is yin and yang
water and air
It is life
It is life
life
She smiled when she said it
He drove
so far
faster

                                        In the end there were
                                        tears more words
                                        The road reduced to
                                        broken slab
                                    the grass growing through
                                        His father said
                                        Never
                                        stop the car
                                        until you arrive
                                    where you have been going

135

A poem begins as
a lump in the throat,
a sense of wrong,
a homesickness,
a lovesickness.

Robert Frost

Janna Schledorn

YESTERDAY

Did you see the eclipse?
The cable guy came to fix the internet.
Three bags of groceries stacked on the kitchen floor.
A small bowl of pistachios and a mug
of zinfandel and cranberry juice.
My brother-in-law drives away in a bright blue
convertible with his inheritance check.
Seven women discuss *Lessons in Chemistry*.
Dirty dishes in the sink, cat pee on the porch.
Did I tell you they hired my replacement?

Cigar Workers' Houses, Tampa   by Marc Davidson

Suncoast Writers Guild
Poetry Pod

Kenny Charnell

COFFEE LOST

I lost my cup of coffee.
I know it's somewhere
here within the house.
It was nice and hot and steamy.
It tasted so delicious as it
sloshed inside my mouth.

My cellphone could be sitting next to it.
Wherever that may be?
If I should locate the two of them
I might also find my keys.

Maybe they're with the remote control?
It would be nice to turn the TV on.
But I'm not sure I would hear it
Because my hearing aids are gone.

I do know where my glasses are.
I feel them sliding down my nose.
If they should get past the end of it,
who knows where they will go?

So… I'll pour another cup of coffee,
and ponder where to search.
Are phone, keys, aides, and coffee altogether?
Or does each have its own mysterious perch?

Ann Favreau

FLOUR SACK SAGA

In Englewood, a long way back
Clothes were made of flour sacks.

That was fine, until the day
Madeline went out to play.

She stood upon the swing of wood
Not knowing that the children could
See her underpants.

Though Mother scrubbed the flour sack,
She couldn't erase the words in black
SELF RISING.

Sister hollered loud and clear,
"Sit down, quick, my Maddie dear,

'Fore all the kids in the neighborhood
Tease your flour panties good!"

Maddie sat down hard and fast,
Vowing that would be the last

She would wear the pants at play.
She'd save them for a special day,

When she would don a pretty dress
And nobody would ever guess

That words caressed her little bum,
SELF RISING.

Tanya Young

HEARTS OUT FOR A RIDE

It's an ordinary morning in June
That smells of clean washing and grass cuttings
Bees riding the summer breeze
As Uncle Thunder and Mrs. Beulah Brown
Take their hearts out for a ride in his old clunker
An angel dancing on the rusty right wheel
Mr. Bob Brown resting between them
Morning gospel blaring from the radio

They pass a little dogwood tree
Losing its mind
Overflowing with blossoms
Its feet chanting

The car comes to rest
High on a mountaintop
Mrs. Beulah takes her husband in her hands
He's ash now, like the finest sand
She rubs some on her skin
And flies him to the face of God

What happens to old love?
Tell me if you know

Sunshine Poets

Cheri Neuman Herald

REFLECTIONS IN A PUDDLE

Day after day we woke to warm rain drumming the corrugated
roof. Lying long past the
alarm, fingers lingering along the lines of each other. Heat steam-
ing windows open to the night.

Day after day we woke to green rain sliding down fat banana
leaves, tickling spider webs
inch by inch. Heaven reflected in a puddle by the door.

Henry Flagler's dream railroaded our town. Sand is no place for
deep roots when paradise is
parceled into feet instead of acres and concrete cloverleafs re-
place the greener kind.

We saw it coming, concrete mile by mile but did nothing except
complain and watch the papers.

Old Henry's trains still run, bring pockets full of money with the
tourists, the transplants and their
sunshine dreams, to the bloated land of plenty. We took the train
to the mountains, bought a simple
piece of highland dream—tin-roofed with a wrap-around porch—
and waited for soothing rain.

"Poetry is an echo,
asking a shadow to dance."

Carl Sandburg

Kenneth P. Hughes

DREAMONS AND DEMONS

The day is done, the night has won,
and satisfied, I rest,
When once again you visit me,
And put me to the test.

We ended thirty years ago.
The spirit in us died,
Or so I thought. But in my mind
You found a place to hide.

Yet all the good times now return.
The bad is swept away.
Remembering what we once had,
we have again today.

The dreamons of my mind awake
The life we wish we had.
They dance on my imagination:
I'm a younger lad.

Each pad of memory awakens
When the dreamons land,
And you're the same as when I first
Reached out to hold your hand.

And with each step the dreamons dance,
They sweep away the years,
So you and I can be ourselves again,
Without the fears.

The more the dreamons dance and play,
The more I reminisce.
I sleep alive with you again,
A land of peace and bliss.

A paradise I thought was lost
I find until the morn,
When dreamons of the eve
Become my demons of the dawn.

The sunlight fills the room with darkness
In my private lair.
As I awake, my dreamons
are the demons of despair.

Peggy Evans Hughes

THE PERFECT BUBBLE

He nods from across the room.
I nod my response.

He rises and slowly approaches.
As he stands by my chair, I rise.

I stand and fluidly inhale and lift
my breasts, planting them on his chest
as is the thing to do.

I lean forward, weight on my toes
onto his body as he takes a step back.
He leans into my body, forming an apex.

Right hand on my back, a welcome warmth and nothing more.
His left lifts away from his side.
My right delicately lays itself onto his left,
like a coat on a rod.

He takes a breath, tips my weight to his right
And surges forward.

Sternum to sternum,
our communication connection.
I close my eyes.

He picks an instrument
and paints it on the floor with my steps.
Backing, crossing, zig and zag.
Slithering.

He pushes forward,
then suddenly, rocks back.
My left leg involuntarily
does a high kick to my rear.

We circle, my hips tick-tocking
as my upper body stays still…
connected to his sternum.

Each step is a mystery,
unknown, until my center of gravity is tipped.
His chest is my compass. his breath, my plumb.

We stop, pause,
drink in a few beats of the music.
And we are off again.

His moves interpret perfectly
the notes and rhythm.
We float in unison, effortlessly.

We are inside our own sphere of existence.
Living, breathing the music.
Being the music.
Nothing exists outside the perfect bubble.

The 3 minutes are up. The song is done.
I open my eyes.
We smile at each other as we part,
strangers at a dance.

Jinny Kelley

THE COAL BREAKER BOYS

It was the photographer
that caught the boys—
black-faced underground,
cramped in a car.
A wooden box on wheels
in the anthracite coal mines.

There were hours of black sweat...
like Hades down there—the black jungle.
Boys lost their youth, limbs, fingers,
and some lost lives.
8–12 years old on immigrant overtime
without the benefits.
Casualties, because of market prices,
and the heat driving labor too far.
Mothers crying,
pleading for a casket from the company store.

And the coal mining barons
using coal for their stained glass windows
upon mansions on mountain tops—
feeding their furnaces with black diamonds.
Northeastern PA, black rivers running
through mountains fused by glaciers.
The next town over sinking slowly
because of mining,
nothing growing on the hills, mounds
of impurities the boys picked out
many years ago...

Lehigh Valley Coal—
one grandfather in the office,
another down in the mine.
As a young boy, he got out
but left this impression on him.
He always washed his face before dinner,
and put on a clean white shirt.
He washed his hands time and time again,
the black lines that never left—
memories underground
and lungs with residue…

The photographer found light
at the entrance.
The conveyer belt moving up and down
with the boys cramped in box cars,
too young to see—
where morning was night, and night into dawn—
eyes blinded by the light,
a grey sky with the sun behind the clouds.

Angie M. Mayo

THE GRANDSON—A Rondine

Little legs running so, so fast
I'd wait—they'd stop when they reached me
he'd laugh each time with impish glee
pretending this would always last
but now, all's in the distant past.
What I would give to once more see
little legs running.

A grown man now, he has not asked
about his picture at age three
still by the chair I drink my tea
where in my mind I still can cast
little legs running.

The Halifax River at Noon   by Marc Davidson

Tomoka Poets

B. J. Alligood

THE FISHERMAN
(For Dave Bonomi & Mike Manecke)

daily he would plant his feet on shifting sands
as the Atlantic Ocean swirled about his legs

he'd fling the weighted line away from his
body toward an unseen prize hoping for a
flash of silver to snatch the hook and run through
the surf with abandon

he repeated this ballet while the sun sagged behind
his back

when afternoon shadows fell upon the waves
he'd collect his clams, knife, two poles, sand spikes,
and bucket of fish and head home where a
wooden work bench, faded from years in the sun,
awaited his catch

translucent moon-discs would fly through the
air as he scaled his catch and local cats collected
about his feet awaiting the flip of fish heads and offal

the reddened broiler would receive cleanly rinsed fillets
dotted with butter and herbs while the table was laid
with freshly-picked garden vegetables, roasted and
seasoned along with crusty French bread
and cold, breathing wine

the fisherman's reward for his daily efforts

Kenice Broughman, D.C., DHSc

HIDDEN CURVES

As an oversized coat
Disguises the curves underneath
So, my old life
Hid the curves of my being.
Shedding the old fur,
As warm and comfortable as it was,
Signaling new beginnings,
A bud gently unfolding its silky petals,
A beauty unexpected,
In those secret chambers.
A new life begun,
A fresh garment,
Lighter and gilded with
Silken rainbow threads,
It fits my curves and reveals
What lies beneath.
The fit suits me
And I delight
In the freedom of
Becoming me

Gary Broughman

A WOMAN FOR ALL SEASONS

Have you searched for love?
I have.
Did you know what you were
searching for? Or who?
I thought I did, but didn't
know then what I know now.
I was asking much.
Too much?
A woman for all seasons.
Hot as summer when desire
sweeps her away.
Cold and clear-eyed as a crisp winter day
when feeling too much might betray her.
Ready to blossom anew in eternal spring
whenever her heart spots a new horizon,
able to let go like falling leaves
when time has run its course.

How could I have made sense then
of one who walked in such glory?
Me, still trudging through the
deep woods, feet tangled in creeping vines,
lucky to stay upright a few feet, lucky
to find the next foothold, let alone my
way into the open where I too might walk
with easy strides on the well-lit path.

When I did see her, this
woman for all seasons,
youth had passed,
middle age eclipsed
by the steady ticking of the clock,

the body less, the mind more,
and Spirit ripened like fruit
after the first autumn chill.
Would I have seen her sooner had I
not been so blinded by the dense woods?
Could I have peered through the brush,
past the thick trunks of trees
and seen her skipping on the path?
Could I have, with one primal breath,
burst through the choking undergrowth
and cried out, "There you are my love!"
my dream woman who holds for me
all the secrets of beauty's reign on earth,
my woman for all seasons,
and heard her whisper back,
"I've been here on this path,
wondering when you'd arrive."

Or would I have heard her say,
"I only now arrived here myself,
Until this moment I too was tripping
through the dense dark forest."

It could be true,
I believe it so,
that ripeness is all,
that all things happen,
happen only,
in the fullness of time.

Sue-Ellen "Niki" Byram

THIS MORNING'S SUNRISE

This morning's sunrise,
A thin tangerine stripe
Lies parallel to the horizon;
Struggling to rise to make
Its presence known.

Overtop of the awaited, and anticipated,
Colorful arrival, hangs a thick bank of
Dark, bluish-black storm clouds,
Weighing heavy on the day
Like my broken heart.

"Poetry is the art of creating
imaginary gardens
with real toads."

Marianne Moore

Mitzi J. Coats

GATHERING

The countryside spools by
the car windows,
a day's drive
past peanut and cotton fields,
fruit trees peach and pecan,
lying fallow until spring,

between small communities
with old-fashioned names
of long ago founders
and river trade trails
Dothan Opelika Plains

working farms threaded together
by railroad tracks and a red light
a convenience store
faded sign dangling over
gas pumps rusted red
from deep-south humidity,
the coffee hot if too strong.

Still, one sees change –
sleek tractors and late-model cars
on wide paved roads,
modern housing stitched among
the abandoned homesteads
their chimneys crumbling
above viny bondage

and arriving at the reunion,
I find a family woven so tightly together,
a well-worn, warm blanket
of people, place, and time
wrapped around my shoulders,
as to ward off any chill
of the past
and furrow fresh ground for the future.

Sonja Jean Craig

ANGELIC SOUL ADRIFT

Copper Medusa watches
digital waves sweep the Earth
that commands and controls minds,
irritates empty hearts,
grasps for links.

Conduit of emotion —
giver of indwelling life,
illuminates her show-stopping love
to humans — sucked in
by their phones.

Compassion's eye radiates
reflections of ancestors
alive in the ethereal.
Made physical in metal veins
hidden between solar flares
and full moon salutations.

She wears a multitude of orbs.
Shaped by brilliance —
electrically charged by purity,
magnetized by grace.
Seen only by those who
want to see veiled miracles.

Colleen O'Leary

WIND OF TIME

Another year has
come and gone
Too soon the
months blow by
Caught in a turbulence
of aging wind
reflection I barely
recognize.
Withered and worn
spots of age now
show how old man
time has caught up to
me so bold.
Spinning into a
whirlwind of cracks
and creeks, bones
that do not reach.
Vision blurred with
clouds of gray
with no idea of
what I say.
While memories grow
distant in my mind,
it's only a matter of time.
Feeling the wind just
a faint breeze upon
my face, now realizing
it was not the wind
but the last breath
I take.

Joseph Perrone

MY SPOUSE, MY LOVER, MY FRIEND

In the beginning, with our love aflame,
We knew that our lives would ne'er be the same;
'Cause our hearts that afore beat separately
Then, and thereafter, as one beat jointly.

For, just like the light that captured the moth,
We captured our love and so pledged our troth,
Hoping forever a life full of love
With prayers for a marriage blest from above.

And so we were joined soulmates forever,
Bound by a love that no one could sever
While knowing beginnings someday would end;
That the ties that us bind one day could rend.

Now, near the end, loving words are spoken,
Knowing bonds of love will ne'er be broken
'Cause our souls live on for eternity,
Where you and I together ere will be.

And if I leave first I know you'll abide,
For, with time, once more you'll be at my side
Where all new beginnings never will end;
My spouse, my soulmate, my lover, my friend.

Rose, Leu Gardens   by Elaine Person

Pamela Ramey Tatum

GUILT

Unmoved
by my sorrow
you sit at the piano
waiting for me to speak,
wanting a confession—
errors
missteps
guidance not taken

Your eyes
shards of glass
cut through me—
I turn away
You bang
on the keys—
a violent cacophony

After
in the long silence
I hear you break
look back
see your eyes
softened

Still
you stare at me
like a hungry child
begging

There
in the lingering smell
of oranges
and my blood-stained
lavender dress
I have the knowing
my guilt
over our loss
is a ghost
that will never
leave.

Breakfast Meeting   by Pamela Ramey-Tatum

FSPA Members at Large

Patricia Barry

THE ELVIS DREAM

In my dream last night, a young woman with long brown hair
stood with her back to me in a store.
The place was silent.
We were both barefoot.

She held up and examined Elvis Presley fifties-style shirts
with rolled-up short sleeves and his image on the front.
I was mentally picking out the top I wanted
as she inspected first the snowy white tees and then
the more dramatic black blouse.

My dream ended before either of us chose a shirt,
though we were both drawn to the mostly black one
with a collar that could stand up
and a small color print of Elvis' face on the chest pocket.

No doubt what that girl and I needed were shoes—
blue suede ones to dance in, in the aisles—but
we already had other, more necessary things
like what it took to be happy,
in our youth and dreams then,
as Hound Dog music played in our heads
and time stretched out before us
in a ceaseless summer afternoon
while we were choosing the essential
Elvis shirt.

Susan Love Brown

DOROTHY'S DILEMMA

Dorothy is caught in an Oedipal dilemma
played out on a yellow brick road.
She worships her father, an emerald wizard,
but rivals her mother's witcherly ways.

Like Solomon, she solves her problem
by splitting her mother in two:
one white and pure full of love and sparkle,
one green in black with clawed nails and no clue.

Dorothy dances in ruby red slippers,
seducing scarecrows, tinmen, and lions.
Flaunting sexuality without a way home,
She dances through poppies and sleeps off her high.

Alas, in true fashion of girls coming of age,
she kills half a mother with water and rage,
only to watch her fine father float up and away
in his beautiful unstoppable fire-powered balloon.

Dorothy decide: an adventurer be
and get carried away on the winds of a dream,
or return like a drudge to the dust bowl of Kansas
to a place called no-place-like-home.

Hanh Chau

MY FAVORITE COOKIE

A delicious taste of cookie
indulge with hunger crave
for a sweet tooth of desire
from a grandma's baking
permeate kitchen stage
fill with emotion display
that comes with a wide
an array of decorative
design for special guests made
A cup of chocolate milk
add to give a perfect match
for the lunch snack treat
at the spending moment
It embraces the heart of joy
elated smile put on a face
a lullaby singing a song to play
with a rejoicing of celebrating
of a story-telling time memory
from a family holiday gathering

B. Shawn Clark

SHOO FLY!

Once Upon a Time
I would always rhyme

There would be glints in an eye
Or a pie in the sky

Then came a fly

In the ointment

Such disappointment!

Then one fine day
I found a new way

The verse was free
But not for me

The way had a cost:
A poet's soul lost

Florida Bred Standard Poodle   by Kenice Broughman

Linda Marie Cossa

CONSOLATION

Inspired by Andrew Rudin's Sonata for Violoncello & Piano

with all this grief
I am asking you what to do

I asked a drum what to do
he said "touch me touch me until spirit flows free"

I asked a fiddle what to do
he said "kick your heels, stomp your feet, make it reel"

I asked a violin what to do
she said "sound near ear heart listening"

I asked a guitar what to do
she said "gut instincts touch heart strings"

I asked a harp what to do
and that precious child said
"hold me, sing me a lullaby tune"

I wonder what a cello would say or do?
I do believe
it would speak some kind of innate infinity

       some indigenous love
       in the heart of humanity

Timothy S. Deary

CATS

The cat made himself comfortable on the roof
                              of the old brown house,
completely at ease,
almost asleep and perfectly steady.

We wondered, "How did he get up there?"
Amazed at his balance and imagining the acrobatics
                    that it must have taken to get up there.

Over at the barn the orange cat made his presence known
                              with loud vocalizations,
once he had your attention he rubbed against your legs
                              and purred loudly.

Then there was the black and grey striped cat,
more content to lounge on the barn floor, occasionally
                    flicking his tail at an annoying fly.

(he looked like he was contemplating a nap before the heat
                    of the day became unbearable.)

Rory was curled up by the side of the bed,
tail curled around her, asleep,
no doubt she won the latest round of chase with the dog,
using her own acrobatics to get by her again,
having won,
she was content.

Cats with climbing skills,
acrobatic felines at home high above the ground,
cats who are friendly and welcoming,
purring loudly for a bit of affection,
cats, content to nap and rest as the day heats up,
an occasional flick of the tail,
eyes half closed,
cats, content to get the best of the dog,
then celebrate in deep sleep in fading summer light.

Melody Dean Dimick

BLOSSOMING

Many days, I've been an Emily Dickinson line.
Poets, you know the one, beginning
"I'm Nobody! Who are you?"
That's not me now.

In today's fantasy, I'm whimsical:
a mesmerizing mermaid, somebody swimming
in Weeki Wachee's cool, crystal-clear spring,
enchanting children and other tourists.

My parents do not understand why
I want to escape to the world of Florida
Disney characters, spared from Wall Street
woes, bankruptcies, COVID, and job losses.

I dream of colorful cinematic frames.
But Mother doesn't care;
she doesn't value goals I hold dear.
To succeed, I must fit her corporate mold.

No sense arguing with her.
The disappointment in her eyes,
the contempt in my father's frown,
the check written to Stanford University

tell me my words fall on deaf ears.
But I'll break free from expectations.
I won't fit into someone else's vision.
I'll be the flower, not the STEM

Sara Gipson

SNOWY EGRET PHOTOGRAPHS

I watch snowy egrets glide
like kites along slow currents
where air flows above the lake.

My camera lens captures
a dancer's grace, white wings spread
to shadow boats racing time.

I come to this lake to fish.
I reel in real beauty, peace,
and amazing photographs.

Mary Rogers-Grantham

THE SOUL OF RAIN
a Persona Poem

Under the arc of sky, weather howls.
I weep with regret, like bounced lost
love hungry for evaporated words.
Another broken day full of tears

answering grounds of green grass, and
watering hills of blue-green junipers
to the music of my elements that ride
in the wake of winds while crossing

seasons where rivers wave and ambush
dark. Under the shelter of sky, in the arms
of trees, I labor through pitching clouds
weeping, wringing out my soul in hymns.

Nina Heiser

WE SING EACH OTHER HOME

I watch the mockingbird dart
from the purple bougainvillea
to the magnolia so spare
this spring but there she perches
twig in beak waiting a beat
and then back she dashes
building a nest inside those
thick and thorny branches

women in the city wait
a while before they
turn on the lights
don't want anyone
who might be watching to know
which window they call home

the mocker swoops to grab
a strand of Spanish moss
a twig broken off a dying tree
to build a safe place
deep in the recesses
of wild flowering vine

she stands guard
at the edge of the roof
I too
have learned to be aloof
we're good I tell her
for now
but the songs
we sing are not our own

Gordon Magill

TORNADO

Dawn
thunderclap
booms cannon shot loud
trees stir uneasily
pale early light dims to dark
electric crackling of lightning
glowing blue
within the gloom
a growing rushing river of wind
rain darts horizontally in silver arrows
we leap from bed to window in alarm
instantly it is upon us on every side
enfolded within the banshee wings
of an angel of death we scream
in terror
all is roaring wind hurricane force
rainwater whipped into white foam
our little house a boat overwhelmed
by great waves of blinding sea and dragged down
racing from window-to-window unbelieving
feeling death's icy breath upon our necks
pistols bang and rifles crack
as branches give way and fly
grenades and mortars explode
as trees break crashing all around
the house shudders as a trunk hits the roof
encircling vortex of wind lashes our sheltering forest
into submission…then instantly…silence

the demon storm races on
rain now vertical gushes down
the greenish gloom fades
to morning misted light
no sound no birds no wind
trembling with shock
we warily open doors
to peer out at
devastation

Sharon McKenzie

PEACE

Emotions ripple with the desire for stillness
Calm found in small places, quiet places away from others
Yet the pull of mankind is strong
I say, don't waste your strength on me
Let me find my solace for it is the ugliness I cannot bear
The repetitive destruction of ourselves
Have we learned nothing in 3000 years?
Why must we fight and kill?
Why is power and money so important?
When all we really want is love…and peace.

Glenn Erick Miller

(NOT) ONLY IN FLORIDA

It's not only in Florida
where neighbors go crazy,
wear pajamas to church,
and wrestle man-sized reptiles (for fun).

It's not only in Florida
where teens surf in a hurricane,
hurl hot dogs at cops
and impersonate doctors
and lovers.

It's not only in Florida
where men confess to murdering their make-believe friends
and break back into prison
to visit their real ones.

But it might be only in Florida
where people shoplift parrots,
hunt pythons for bounty,
steal floating tiki bars and Segways,

tattoo "Flo-Grown" on their fingers,
wrestle gators (for money),
build bridges over oceans,
build fences for the panthers,

and come to plant their toes
in the white sands of paradise,
hiding at the reposed lower lip
of America.

Mary Ellen Orvis

DOWNHILL

It's just a fact of life.
No matter what apologists and purveyors
of forgiveness insist,
some mothers just don't love their kids.
Caught unaware, in a bind, misunderstood,
kids a nuisance, nothing cute about them:
a real pain.

Like the facts of life,
drawn on a blackboard covered by a sheet,
until the nun explains about blood and babies,
and after class you drop a nickel in the machine
on the girls' bathroom wall, turn the handle,
watch drop a box with a thick cotton pad
that attaches by end tails to hooks on elastic straps
you wear underneath your pants.

For years celibate women preach the art of love to you.
Boys forbidden territory, girls together never imagined.
Watch out, they warn, pray and practice holiness.
Stay a virgin, wear a white dress.
Create a family after being chosen,
like a commodity on the chastity conveyor belt.

What an impossible burden!
But shun it at your own risk.
Those my dear are the true facts of life,
and after that it's all downhill.

John Pryor

AND STILL, THEY DANCE

They don't dance as once they did
There is no Jitter in their Bug
No East or West Coast to their Swing
Just Ohio if they can make it
Their Salsa is very mild
Their Tango is timid
Their Meringue made with low fat cream
Where once they Waltzed, they wobble
Their Fox can no longer Trot
And yet they rise
Go out on the floor
And, when others
Who in foolish fear stay seated…
They dance.

Dennis Rhodes

ANOTHER RESTLESS NIGHT

Time steals away with flowers.
Time leaves us few delights.
It uproots trees with fierce storms.
It tells beloved dogs to go
away. Men like myself are
born to be disillusioned.
O God, I do not know what else
to do but pick up my pen
and keep trying, keep trying
to conjure up a better world!
Time has stabbed me in the heart
but it has kept on beating.
Give me poetry, never a rose.
I know too well what time does with those.

Evelyn Ann Romano

LILA HALL IN THE MORNING

Lila Hall is a YOGA studio in Costa Rica

Awake, she hurls kisses at the mountains
and steps carefully to Lila Hall.

The room is silence, the teacher serenity,
birdsong and love the only sounds.

She starts to breathe and begins the
gentle movements to open the body.

Her heart is light and she is fully present.

A change occurs as barriers melt
and flowing flowers invade the space.

She surrenders to this with joy and gratitude.

The mountains smile and she invites them
in to share her last Om.

Daniel Stone

I BREATHE IN

My world was crumbling
as I filled my lungs with survival
surrendering to the suffocating ocean air.
Breathing in I gasped like a dying man
taking in more life than seemed available.

Angry skies stretch across the horizon
thunder explodes as clouds expand
moving in choking out the blue sky.
Oncoming the storm is moving for landfall
about to send water over the beach seawalls.

High tides and flooding
hurricane winds with a huge storm surge.
Catastrophic damage predicted to area homes
"Take cover, Take cover" seek shelter now.
All beach side overpasses to the mainland will close.

Now I am panting like a over worked sled dog.
Gasping for life giving air in my panic.
"Stop it" the end may not be near yet.
"Get a grip" I tell myself loudly.
Quietly I say, you have experienced this before so,
I Breathe In

Christine Valentine

SHROVE TUESDAY

Oft-times it rained.
But it was warm indoors
with the gas burner flaring
and the frying pan heating
for a feast, before the fast
of Lent.

She made a pile of pancakes
then came toward the table
pan in hand, and we waited
with baited breath.

A quick toss along with
a back and forth motion,
and the pancake flew up high,
flipped over, and returned to the pan
upside down. *Do it again, Mum*
Do it again. So she grinned
and repeated it for us several times.
Now eat your pancakes she said,
showed us how to squeeze lemon juice
on it and sprinkle with granulated sugar.

Each Shrove Tuesday
I still miss the aroma
of the seared batter,
the fragrant bite of fresh lemon,
the crunch of the sugar.

Tanya R. Whitney

DEATH OF AUTUMN

There is an unearthly stillness
Unlike yesterday's vibrant air.
No movement or activity,
Only an eerie sense of death.

White snowy flakes of death fall down
Upon the cold, weathered terrain.
Like a volcanic storm of ash,
It leaves a desolate landscape.

Like a widow's black mourning veil,
Her sorrow and grief are covered.
The vast landscape is enveloped
With a burial shroud of white.

There is no longer any warmth
In the hearth of nature's power.
There is only the rising tide
Of frozen waves of its demise.

The twilight of life's sunset when
The harvest of the soul begins,
To rest in a season of sleep,
The winter of one's existence.

Carol Wilson

BLANK PAGE

I wake up with the greatest love poem
Written in my mind while gazing at your
Lovely back curled beside me
And as sleep claims me and tosses me into
Conscious thought
That poem waves goodbye
And here I am
Late at night
Cheesecake baking
Smelling heaven while you
Read next to me.
We sit now as a pajamaed couple.
Love grows as you turn a novel's pages
And I stare at a poemless blank page

Swan and Coot   by Nancy K. Hauptle MacInnis

FSPA Contest Winners

1. FSPA Free Verse Award

Mary Ellen Orvis
Sun City Center, FL

WOMEN'S DAY MARCH, NYC, 1975

I remember how we shimmered in columns,
down the open avenues, banners proclaiming equality.
Our chants crashed through concrete canyons
carrying forward a future we could only imagine,
In solidarity with women's struggles worldwide.

Onlookers taunted us, cursed our steps,
while we kept silent, looking upward,
invoking Athena, goddess of war and reason,
to guide and protect our quest.

Now I know.
If we had wanted to silence those fools,
we should have lifted our skirts,
shown them those secret silent mouths,
our terrifying power that men cannot understand.

2. FSPA Formal Verse Award
Petrarchan Sonnet

Diane Neff
Longwood, FL

I KNEW A WOMAN

The floor beneath her feet was dirt, hard packed
by leather workmen's boots on tired feet.
She swept and dusted, keeping home a sweet
refuge for her man, held their bond intact.
Her wood stove warmed the house with love, the pact
they'd made long years before, in haste, in heat,
had never wavered. Each breath, each heartbeat
renewed commitment to their lives' contract.

I knew this woman once, before she died,
in luxury, she claimed – smooth boards of oak
her floor – she sanded, polished 'til they shone.
The stove – electric – grilled and baked and fried,
yet nothing matched the smell of hickory smoke
and love still strong in memory, all else gone.

3. The Live Poets Society Award

Carlton Johnson
Winter Park, Florida

& AFTER THE DARKNESS ABATED
after Brenda Hillman

It's dark out
      and yet not so
my eyes move about
      picking up cold embers
      of light, mere
memories falling in front of my eyes
like sleet on an absent afternoon.

Not even a moon
though perhaps it is shrouded
behind some bank of star-stealing clouds,

perhaps,

and yet, even as I struggle
to see, there is a glow
everywhere. More precisely,
the east, as the first rays
collide with my retina
sensing my place
in the universe.

"Poetry: the best words in the best order."

Samuel Taylor Coleridge

Cheryl A. Van Beek
Wesley Chapel, FL

QUEEN HIPPOCAMPUS

Inside a glassy cube, a Queen
wears the forever crown she was born with.
Her genus bears the same name
as the part of our brains
that births memories, Hippocampus.
The 2-inch-long, once live, seahorse rules
a kingdom of Fort Lauderdale souvenirs floating
in a sea of the past.

A breen-colored wishbone of seaweed
drapes the Queen's back like a velvet cape.
A purple-spired snail and beaded, gold
periwinkle bejewel her throne.
A fortress of sun-bleached, coral cactus
guards the palace.

In the Queen's water garden, a white Coquina shell
flashes the rose hue that blooms in its hollow.
What I see depends on how I tilt the cube.
Trinkets and truths flip, overlap.

I'm drawn into her stilled gaze,
eyes that once could see separately—
forwards and backwards simultaneously.
I look back to the beach we strolled, the ocean we swam,
the hotel shaped like a giant ship.

Water and time, displace, reveal, hide.
I envision her steadying herself,
her tail spiraling a blade of seagrass.

Decades since those childhood vacations,
I cringe to learn that each year, about a million seahorses
are pulled from oceans for the souvenir trade.

My mind sways, anchors in hope that my seahorse
just washed up with the waves.
I lock my treasure box of memories.
In honor of the tiny Queen,
shells slide, collide,
make music like a lapping tide.

5. Willard B. Foster Memorial Award

Grace Diane Jessen
Glenwood, UT

DRIVING LESSON

"Now, Daughter, look behind you,
make sure the way is clear.
I'm sitting right beside you
so there's no need to fear."

"Oh, Daddy, I'm so nervous,
but I will do my best
to follow your instructions
and drive as you request."

"Then check the rear-view mirror,
put the car into reverse,
back down the driveway slowly –
too fast! There's nothing worse!"

"I'm glad no cars were coming,
but we made it to the street
and barely touched the trash can.
Where's the pillow for my seat?"

"It's here. Can you see better?
Then let up on the brake
and go down to the corner
and turn right. Heaven's sake!"

"Oh, dear! I know I should have
made sure which gear I'm in
before I pressed the gas feed,
but is backing up a sin?"

"Calm down. Let's try it over.
Here we go, stay on the right.
Slow down where kids are playing,
Watch out! You ran that light!"

"I'm sorry, Dad, I'm looking
at everything I can.
How much are you expecting
me to do? I'm not a man."

"I'm sorry, too, for yelling,
but I'd like to stay alive.
Let's go back home. Your Mother
can teach you how to drive."

6. The Jock G. and George K. Terry Award

Kathryn (Kit) Schmeiser
Fairview, NC

EVERYWHERE

Back in the *Old Days,* before people
scanned QR codes, typed on miniscule cell
phone key pads, a skinny kid pedals her second-
hand bicycle. Everywhere. She rides over
cracked neighborhood sidewalks, races
down Water Tower Hill. Wind cools
her hair, sun tans her skin.

Long legs bend, straighten. Sneakered
feet grip rubber pedals. Rhythmic up, down
propel girl and bicycle. Metal-rimmed wheels
spin faster. Faster. Everywhere.
Wheels stop.

Her foot pushes the kickstand down,
the bicycle slants sideways at rest. Out
of breath. She runs up wooden stairs, steps
into the old house. A library. Books squeezed
in shelves surround her. The scents of old
wood and paper pages perfume her hair,
her clothes. The girl fingers book spines,

opens chapters. She piles worn stories
on a counter – a hidden staircase mystery,
a little house in the woods, a wild black
stallion.

The bicycle waits patiently, sunbeams
warming its padded leather seat. Waiting
for her return, books dropping in a wire
basket hanging on handlebars. Waiting
for a ride home, a quick stop at Jack's
Market for an orange Creamsicle.
Waiting as she wipes melted ice cream
off her chin. Waiting to go.
Everywhere.

7. JUNE OWENS MEMORIAL AWARD

Stephanie DuPont
Sugar Hill, GA

A DAY LIKE THIS

Endless cycles start to what end?
Tiny creatures.   making little worlds
in tide pools.   Microcosms, washed away,
spring to life each day   find fault
in clear nothing,   look
at perfect spirals in shells.   The cosmic energy,
light watching over   curly starfish
and other celestial wanderers   too small to see. The water,
knowing the clouds,   when the waves will hit,
drops of rain fall.   Down temporary canyons
in the sand,   the palm trees swaying,
grass making waves   on land. Distant,
the lighthouse   talking to the sky.
Circles   of families and friends
wax and wane   with the surf.
The ocean,   longing to be caressed.
The comfort   of floating, warmth,
sun on face. Tangled   seaweed, now
scratching skin.   Timeless. Tides
eating sandcastles,   driftwood
going back to nostalgia.   Why are stones round?
The horizon   draws a line.
To swim,   to feel,
the subdued sounds   of sunset,
to inhale   the breeze,
knowing   there's a last time,
the sandpiper   still flies,
to its nest   at night.
Whatever's   holding us
sleeps. And so, the moon   binds us tightly
to our memories, earth.   Where every end
is a prelude to a new start.

8. New River Poets Award

John Michael Sears
Daytona Beach, FL

LINE, POINT, CIRCLE: THE SHAPES OF TIME

sluggish time, I thought, would travel as straight as my Schwinn,
coasting the hard clay path beside the train tracks toward
where the Spanish War's gray-beards sat with bootleg whiskey
as they gathered each Saturday around their chessboards
in the town square – I'd search for my usual shady spot
to watch their tournaments while struggling to look at ease
as they swore oaths and drank from bottles in paper bags –

time, they told me, slowed down under magnolia trees,
but hourly, they would check their silver pocket watches,
and nod to themselves, agreeing with the clock's brass bells –
then dipped their powdered snuff staining their beards brown
or re-lit Kaywoodies when wanting that sultry Cuban smell.

in my teens, closed cotton mills forced families to leave,
and chess-playing old vets were crowded out of downtown
by the addicts and the homeless begging for their meals,
while litter, like playful mice, scurried the courthouse grounds
amid rusting parking meters that were no longer in use –
even if neglect hadn't stopped the clock's antique wheels,
the nearly empty streets with boarded-up stores
verified that there's a point when time indeed stands still.

of course, the town changed again, pleasant now, gentrified,
like a wrinkled old man decked out in trendy attire,
with its crowded antique shops and vibrant art boutiques,
plus a new park with everything skateboarders desire,
while each hour loud speakers play recorded, soothing chimes
from the tower's new electric clock, designed to please
old snowbirds, like myself, who visit the town each spring
on our migration from winter homes in the Keys
in search of cool breezes at our lake cabins in Maine –
an annual cycle that spins faster than those bike wheels
that conveyed me past the sweet fragrance of magnolias,
where falsehoods about the slowness of time seemed so real.

9. The Poet's Vision Award

Lisa Kamolnick
Blountville, TN

AGNOSTICATION

"Hell is truth known too late." — J.C. Ryle

A tiger-totem *Life-of-Pi*-ness
lies beneath my awkward shyness.
Which way should I genuflect?
Or should I merely sit erect?
Palms together? Up? Apart?
On lap? In air? Pressed at my heart?
Inside a whale, with white-winged bird,
I seek the wisdom of the Word.
I sit inside my monkey mind
in theological unwind:
Mother, chants, runes, Rah,
blood of lamb, śavāsana,
nirvana, tarot, yin or yan,
Buddha, Yahweh, Son of Man?
God of Mercy, Embodied Light—
Oh, Jesus! Was Muhammad right?
Eye of newt and wing of dove,
I hold this true: where God is—is love.

Zen Coquina   by Sonja Jean Craig

10. Alfred Von Brokoph Award

Marianne Peel
Lexington, KY

TROUBLESHOOTING

Who will clean up after the hailstorm?
Who will spackle the dents in the siding?
Who will bump out the pitted places
    in hood of my father's car?
No knick-knacks or fuzzy dice
    tangled and suspended from his rearview mirror.
No plastic Jesus propped on the windshield,
    magnet affixing the crucifix to the dashboard.
My father prefers the cardboard Jesus,
    propped up in every room of the house
    or nailed to the wall, always pounded into the stud.
Our house refused to be a public place.
Visitors downright tentative to sit, to slouch, to slump
in this museum of a home. I wanted friends
to kick off their shoes, to flop on the sofa.
To pound out Beatles songs with their paradiddle hands
dueling on the cushions. To braid each other's hair
making elephant ear circles ala Princess Leia of Star Wars'
    fame.
Instead, all of our clocks are set to military time.

I remember my father pulling our Sunday drive car
    to the shoulder
to silence a rattle, to adjust a whining vehicle part.
    Remember him
grooming his car grill with the smooth side of the
    chamois cloth.
Remember how he plunged his hands into the Goop jar,
rubbing his mechanic palms together, banishing all evidence

214

of grease or sludge. He was so proud of his clean, clean
    garage.
He'd always said, *You could eat off this floor.*

Today, from a flip phone in Charleston, South Carolina,
my ninety-year-old father tells me that he wants to pour
a gallon of gasoline over his head
and set his body on fire. Tells me the bugs
are just too much. How they crawl under his skin,
swim and squirm in his blood. How he can feel them
burrowing under his wrists, his elbows, his calves,
his everywhere. Tells me how he tries to avoid
scratching them. How they itch and twitch
just under his flesh. How he gouges his skin
in the night, when they are most active.
Tells me he wakes in bedsheets
weeping in blood.

11. Janet Binkley Irwin Memorial Award

Terry Jude Miller
Richmond, TX

NOLAN ROAD NOTEBOOK

Shell and gravel carry father's name
like a concert of commands, a list
of chores repeated in a homily of hunger.

At roadside, blackberry bushes twist in barb wire,
strangle each other. The sun guffaws
at our sling blades and sweaty backs.

A lone oak tree planted by sharecroppers
offers the only shade for a mile in both directions.
Dust ingrains wherever skin creases.

Grass grows back after dying in winter,
summer its festival, fall its cremation—brothers
follow with drenched burlap the flames
their father's set.

Siblings outrun the fire line before
it curdles creosote fence posts,
before it reaches the highway
that runs everywhere away from here.

"Breathe-in experience,
breathe-out poetry."

Muriel Rukeyser

12. KATE KENNEDY MEMORIAL AWARD

Cheryl A. Van Beek
Wesley Chapel, FL

THE CHOCOLATE TASTER

She inhales its roasted aroma, prolongs
her craving, then breaks off a hunk. The snap
means it's well tempered,
promising a slow melt. Fingers glide,
admire hints of its flavor prism—
the sheen from unseen cocoa butter crystals
perfectly aligned inside.
She warms it in her hand,
breathes in the moment, the scent
of celebration, rainforest.

She chews, lets cocoa butter melt.
It tames the tang, velvets her mouth.
She meditates on its bittersweet thrum
rolls the nub, touches each corner of her tongue,
laps its satin nuances, fudgy edges,
deep as the shadow of a Cacao tree.

Her tongue teases out truffle-earthiness,
presses it to the roof of her mouth,
creams it inside her cheeks like ganache—
conches its smoked, buttery rhythm.
Whiffs of nut and java,
her palate peels flavor layers—
some sharp as the machetes that hack open its pods.
Others are dulcet notes she can't name, ripening,
in her mouth, unfurling
like petals of Cacao's tiny white flowers.
She tastes the land where it grew –

218

Madagascar, Ghana, or Peru,

savors the sunbaked terroir,
of hand harvested beans from their pods,
an Ecuadorian understory,
bananas sharing their soil,
orchids climbing their branches.

Silk glides to the back of her mouth.
She closes her eyes, lets it linger,
shivers just before she swallows.
Flavor and memory flood her body. Her spirit
rises to meet them.

13. Henrietta and Mark Kroah Founders Award

Grace Diane Jessen
Glenwood, UT

WONDERING AT A WEDDING

Their granddaughter was married today
in the shade of tall oaks and maples
as a gurgling stream competed
with the minister's voice.
Overhead, two long white lines
crossed a leaf-framed circle of sky.

I hoped her grandparents, long since gone,
were allowed a brief return
to watch her walk with her father
slowly down the forest path.
They may have stood unseen
at the clearing's edge, witnessed
love and joy in the groom's dark eyes
as he took her hands in his.

Perhaps they kissed her cheek,
whispered a wish for happiness
as a flute's clear notes lingered
in the leaves, a white dove left
its cage, flew above the couple,
and rested on an upper branch
of the tallest tree.

14. Past Presidents Award

Janet Watson
Wesley Chapel, FL

HYPNAGOGIA

The encounters arrive unexpectedly,
between wakefulness and sleep,
bringing phantasma that balance lightly
on the thin ledge of consciousness.

Before I drop into the deep,
each swift and transitory vision
or sound carries me
through a sensory surrealism where
      girls in red dresses,
            the lyrics of a pirate chanty,
                  or a plate of macaroni
challenge rational awareness.

These never seem to drift into dreams,
so may only represent the shuffle
of my mind-
      remembering,
            enhancing,
                  discarding,
but these *in transitu* events are well-known
and said to impart sparks of genius to
      inventors,
           and artists,
                 and poets.

Choosing to believe
that such benign or bizarre visits
are muses from a resourceful realm,
I keep a tablet at bedside.

I will be prepared
should enlightenment arrive tonight,
as I travel that cryptic passage
from an existence I know
to one shaped in shadow.

Shutta Crum
Ann Arbor, Mi

WHERE THE GOOD DOG SLEEPS

Where the good dog sleeps
    on the weathered step
Where the day's last light strokes
    the good dog's ear
Where autumn drapes a golden shawl
    over the treetops
Where the last of the garden slumps
    into the deepening twilight
Where birds rise to roost from com
    from gourds, from plump beans
Where toads and crickets sing praises
    to the coming night
Where evening lifts earthy scents
    up from the bottomlands
Where the homeward path is blessed
    by the holiness of creeks and rivers
Where time smooths the path
    to the threshold of an old house
Where a mountain cradles a home
    with a worn step
    that has known a good dog

Joanne Vandegrift
Alva, FL

PAPER PLATE PEOPLE

Paper plate people

Are my kind of folk

Blue jeans and tee shirts

A wink and a joke

Honest and open

With nothing to hide

Children and family

The source of their pride

Dirt under a nail

Or grease in a fold

God loves working hands

They're true and they're bold

Paper plate people

Accept you as friend

They know where you live

Which church you attend

An 8-hour shift

Earns all that they need

Time spent with family

More precious than greed

Mobiles for castles

A used pick-up truck

Outsiders might think

They're down on their luck

The salt of the earth

Strength of God's steeple

Their hearts are pure gold

Paper plate people

16. Leslie Halpern Memorial Award

B. J. Alligood
Cape Canaveral, FL

A gentle boy, with soft and silken locks,
A dreamy boy, with brown and tender eyes,
A castle-builder, with his wooden blocks,
And towers that touch imaginary skies.
– "The Castle Builder" – by: Henry Wadsworth Longfellow

THE DREAM GIVER
(a Gloss poem)

A gentle boy, with soft and silken locks,
Was born to her, a woman all alone.
She raised him well and taught him how to read,
To be successful, when he's fully grown.
She gave him all the tools she thought he'd need.
A gentle boy, with soft and silken locks,

A dreamy boy, with brown and tender eyes,
He found a girl and wooed her for his wife.
A home she wanted, for a wedding gift.
He promised all she wanted in this life
Would be hers in all manner fast and swift,
A dreamy boy, with brown and tender eyes,

A castle-builder, with his wooden blocks,
He made her dream come true in steel and bricks.
They filled their home, with shouts and squeals of kids.
For her, there was nothing he couldn't fix.
For her, there was no thing he would forbid.
A castle-builder, with his wooden blocks,

And towers that touch imaginary skies
Were built for her, beyond the stars and moon,
For her to own the heavens far above.
No thing at her feet, could he lay too soon.
He gave her this, and more with all his love,
And towers that touch imaginary skies.

17. Humor Award

Grace Diane Jessen
Glenwood, UT

AFTER THE FALL

A fall on the ice
     at age eighty-five
left Grandpa impressed
     that he's still alive.

His bruised legs are weak.
     His knees are so sore
he wonders if he
     can walk to the door.

It hurts to sit down;
     it's worse to stand up.
He leans his chair back
     and asks for a cup.

"Don't fall," warned the doc.
     Gramps should have obeyed
for now he's in pain
     and wishing for aid.

He prays to improve,
     says healing's in sight.
He must get well quick—
     he bowls Thursday night.

18. Childhood Award

Marc Davidson
Ormond Beach, FL

LITERATURE

"Our black ship was sailing all over the sea
when we spotted another and shouted with glee.
We prepared to board them and take them all down
as pirates will do, with a sneer and a frown."
        "Write it down."

"The princess would sigh from her tower on high
attracting a prince who was just passing by.
He took a quick sip from his old water flagon
and armed himself well for a fight with a dragon."
        "Write it down."

"Why do you keep saying write it all down?
Writing this stuff is just work for a clown.
I'm just having fun, can't attend to that chore
when I could be telling my friends tales galore."
        "You'll want more."

"You'll want to remember the stories you told
about pirates and dragons and heroes so bold.
If you don't write them down while you have them at hand
you will not remember your stories so grand."
        "If I write…"

"Then your stories, collected, turn into a book
and whenever you want them, you've only to look
for a dragon, a princess, old treasure, new fun,
and then you can share them with everyone."
        "My own book?"

"Your own book, my child, just think of your fame,
when all other children remember your name.
All the stories you told will live on after you.
Write them down for all time – that's the best thing to do."

Marianne Peel
Lexington, KY

TEACH ME TO DANCE BECAUSE BODIES NEVER LIE

He was always the life of the party, my Uncle Harry.
After a few highballs – Cutty Sark and soda – he would kick off
his loafers, loosen his dentures, just a little, and in his stocking
feet, launch into the Buck Time Step on the carpet. He'd make
clicking sounds by rattling his loose dentures. Teeth tapping
against teeth.

My mama put me to bed the night before, pink sponge rollers
plastered to my head, and I was a walking-talking Shirley
Temple holding Uncle Harry's hand tapping out the Alexander
on that rug. My father called Uncle Harry a bullshitter behind his
back. *Dancing is like dreaming with your feet*, my Uncle Harry
used to say.

There was always the promise of Coney Island Amusement Park:
cotton candy on a stick, elephant ears dredged in powdered sugar.
The promise of a Ferris wheel ride after dark. All those lights
winking on the spokes. Sitting in that bucket seat together, lick-
ing cotton candy sugar off our fingers. Calliope music as I
pumped my legs. I longed to swing among the stars, touch my
toes to the edge of the summer moon.

But when we visited him in hospital, he was drenched with night
sweats. White patches on his gums, his tongue, even the lining of
his mouth. Purple splotches on his eyelids. His bourbon belly
gone now. A shriveled up version of himself in a fetal position.
Trying to crawl back into his mama's womb.
But his mama was a wooden spoon kind of woman, hair coiled
in an unyielding bun at the base of her neck. She'd kicked him to
the curb long ago.

Uncle Harry's partner paced the hall outside the hospital room. Monogrammed handkerchief in his jacket pocket. His hands so beautifully manicured. Always such clean and rounded nails. But in his pacing he'd shredded his cuticles. Blood on his knuckles. Hands stuffed into his pockets. So much pacing.

Fluid gathered at the back of Uncle Harry's throat. Raspy voice now, like dry leaves crumpled in his mouth. I served him ice chips from a Styrofoam cup. Offered water on a sponge. Rubbed his feet with aloe and lanolin. Smoothed petroleum jelly between bruised toes.

Cause of death on Uncle Harry's certificate: pneumonia. I knew there was more. Because no one touched the purple sores, his emaciated torso.

Because no one acknowledged the week of diarrhea, the blisters on his cracked lips. Because no one admitted how tired he was. So damn tired.

At the memorial service, all they said about his partner was he made a damn good spaghetti. Meatballs a conglomeration beef and pork. Homemade fettucine. And the basil. So much basil.

And he could dance. Mostly the soft shoe. With a glass of cabernet sauvignon in one hand, his other hand around Uncle Harry's waist. Pasta bowls piled high in the sink.
So close. Dancing. Whistling a made-up tune.
He pulled my Uncle Harry in.

20. Irwin & Estelle Weinbaum Memorial Award

Gary J. Weston
Rice Lake, WI

LIFELINES

Yes, problems plague the world in which we live
With climate fails, false leaders causing dread
But we should still take time to amply give
To those who can't afford some daily bread

Too many in our world lack homes and hope
They do not have a voice that's truly heard
The truth be told, it's tough for them to cope
They have not shared in progress that's occurred

So those of us who have some share of wealth
Should throw a line to those in other boats
And recognize that happiness and health
Must not be rationed via modern moats

It just makes sense to let each other in
And give humanity a chance to win

21. THE ENCHANTMENT AWARD

Stephanie DuPont
Sugar Hill, GA

Dedicated to the unseen, to those who walk the halls of history and imagination, where Nathaniel Hawthorne's pen laid bare the soul of a house—not just haunted, but alive with the spirit of innocent lives taken by ignorance.

THEY SAY THIS HOUSE IS HAUNTED

But all I see are visitors, between the walls
alive, and unafraid.
I watch them come and go,
hear them sing in salted winds,
breathing in tempting lavender and rose.
Do they notice the one shadowed cloud?
"They say this house is cursed;"
Yet, I am the one who's cursed.

Witness the distress of my face,
stained-glass windows darkened with age,
my gloomy clapboard sides.
Hidden in the wilting ferns,
caressing me, slowly strangling.
This place once sheltered lives,
bound by the tales spun beneath my roof.

Malevolence ensnares the seven gables,
slithers down chimneys and dead ashes,
to my solitary table.

I'm drifting in and out—
come in—don't mind my creaking floors—
my weathered doors—decaying bricks—
push through—welcome to the dark—embark—

I persist. I remain.
Climb my secluded staircase if you dare,
The candlelight flickers defiantly in the air.
Nathaniel, are you there?

22. Ekphrastic Poem Award

Carolynn J. Scully
Apopka, FL

SHE KNOWS
*Veiled Lady (*sculpture by Raffaelo Monti of Italy*)*

Crowned with a wreath
of gentle blooms
and veiled behind soft folds,
she is graced to see
beyond the now.

Radiant and peaceful,
surveying the woman
she is today
and will be tomorrow,
her future is not feared.

Behind the mantle,
in her private place,
wisdom befriends her
in the pure silence
and clarity of inner vision.

Midnight Hibiscus   by Shari Yudenfreund-Sujka

23. North Florida Poetry Hub Award

Kenice Broughman
Daytona Beach, FL

ON THE OTHER SIDE

It seems that we are always on the other side of something.
The other side of youth, the other side of work,
Of parenthood, or religion, or opinion,
Of the fence, or the street or the tracks.
Vast gulfs divide us,
Insurmountable differences as tall as the Alps
And as wide as the Pacific,
So that it seems we can never see eye to eye
Or join our hands in an expression of love.

What if there were no chasms of separation,
No thoughts of who is right or who is wrong?
But rather, hearts that, broken open in unity,
Loved without judgement.

Ears that listened and heard the whispers
In the wind of the song
That we all sing,
Just a slightly different tune creating a sweet harmony,
Rather than discordant notes.

The aroma of incense drifting to the heavens,
Frankincense and myrrh,
Blending together to fill the nostrils of heaven
With the scent of one accord.

Eyes that saw beauty in differences,
Like a field of wildflowers
Golden yellow, iris blue, pink and red,
A bouquet of beauty in its variety.

The taste of acceptance on our tongues,
Like a curried melon spicy and sweet,
Bringing out the best in one another.

Our hands joined together forming a chain
Of connection.
The energy of the Divine coursing together,
A river of connection and commitment
To a world we love,
A world to be proud of,
A world for our children to grow and prosper and cherish,
A world where the other side is a mere memory
In the mind of human kind.
A world where your side
Is one with mine.

24. The Look Deeper Award

Margaret Ryan
Tampa, FL

FROST'S RAINY NIGHT

I have listened to the music of your footsteps late at night
Wondering at your artistry—the subtle flow of it,
     the brass-tacks truth of it—

Counterpointing rain-washed streets with distant city lights,
Backdrops for your melancholy and lyric sleights of hand,
Apertures of finely-crafted simplicity,
     housed in sturdy scaffolding,

Oh, I have listened to your silent footsteps one rainy night,
     and heard your
Poetic metronome, weighing life's tempo against
     a shrugging moon

In appreciation for Robert Frost's Poem
"Acquainted with the Night."
The seven lines from Frost's poem:

"I have stood still and stopped the sound of feet
When far away an interrupted cry
Came over houses from another street,

But not to call me back or say good-bye;
And further still at an unearthly height,
One luminary clock against the sky

Proclaimed the time was neither wrong nor right."

25. The Josephine Davidson Memorial Award

Jerri Hardesty
Briarfield, AL

POISONOUS WORDS

The truth has gotten tangled, can't you see?
So many telling lies to you and me,
It's hard to judge which things we can believe
When much of what we hear is fantasy.

The situation makes my stomach heave
To know how some are trying to deceive,
It seems that they will say most anything
To fabricate the tapestries they weave.

And though we know alarm bells loudly ring,
How do we recognize to what to cling?
Without transparency, we are not free.
I fear that this will be the deadly sting.

26. The Book Not The Cover Award

R. M. Williams II
Winter Park, FL

IN THE PRESENCE OF A COMPOSER

The beat is clear against the approaching night,
Drumming in continuation of sunset.
There is no true rhythm,
No metronome.
Only a release of melodies
That has become entwined
in a cove of rock
near the shore.

Then comes a shallow base,
Beating across a red-hazed surface of salt and foam,
A high-pitched note
A wind-blown feather
Mixes in, joins the fray.
Its howling chord
Brushes the overhang of nature,
Echoes blend with waves
Cresting effortlessly in a spray of soul,

As time scales along,
A settling orchestra conducts itself
The swell,
the ebbs,
the flows.
Its cadence of softening cords
Now a moonlight harmony,
Approaching a completed cycle of vocals
in a never-ending solo act
of a chorus born,
And in the silence,
The tenets of the tide
leap in baritone,
Crossing the peaks of sound

240

27. The Homeplace Award

Stephanie DuPont
Sugar Hill, GA

MAPLE STREET

For now, the weathered walls still stand,
fighting tooth and nail to stay rooted.
Peeling paint falling like confetti,
pales with pieces of a mailbox dressed for Christmas,
and this old house lives year-round in my head,
within the bricks—marble galaxies.

Specks of skin, cosmic dust, traces of us
floating in beams of window light.
Winds howling through a sooty chimney,
that burnt wood scent. More than two stories,
overgrown roses filling in the plot,
with plants collected like jewelry—ruby lilies,
treasured cobbled paths welcoming the ivy.
On the porch, the round face of a grandfather clock
keeping watch over frozen thyme.

They remind me of my pulse—
not letting the heart-carved tree or bone-white fence
picketing Maple Street become a ghost.
The golden yearnings of our foundations,
where it breathes, supports our family photographs—
haunted homes, connecting stones to moon.

28. The Suncoast Writers Guild Poetry Pod Award

Diane Neff
Longwood, FL

PONCE DE LEON

Conquistador? Explorer!
In search of youth he sailed.
La Florida was beautiful.
His mission though, he failed.

And time drove on, regardless
of hardships he endured.
His vision fueled his travels;
his dream was not deterred.

Atlantic swells proved hazardous
so Ponce sailed down the shore,
and heading round the keys he sought
a west coast site to moor.

Calusa tribesmen fought him off
but once again he came,
with colonizers for their land
and farming as their game.

Calusa hunters used their bows.
An arrow pierced his thigh.
To Puerto Rico he returned
to live, and then to die.

29. The In Your Own Voice Award

Jonathan Bennett
Lakeland, TN

IN MEDIA ANXIETATIS

there's a crack in the back step 'neath the door
I'm sure with the next freeze will split the house
which will open a space for the roof rats
to get into the bedroom while we sleep
and run all over us and chew the wires
that will start the fire and leave us homeless
living in a poor roach-infested place
with rats which hid in our smoke-smelling clothes
that my wife will leave behind when she goes
before they burn them after I'm locked up
behind a door that's without a handle
like this one that has loosened and come off
through which I cannot escape but can see
there's a crack in the back step 'neath the door

30. The Northwest Florida Poets Award

Holly Mandelkern
Winter Park, FL

THE REMNANTS NEAR THE RYMAN
Nashville, 1920s

The Ryman Auditorium, "Carnegie Hall of the South,"
hosted big stars like Sousa, Houdini, and Chaplin.
Crowds captivated by marches, illusions, and silence
devoured entertainment while feasting on popcorn.
This palace, the "Mother Church of Country Music,"
would decorate the dirt street with ornate arches,
rows of tall windows, and a steeple
pointing skyward, toasting the stars.

Next to this tabernacle stood a mini version
with its small spire, the first house of worship
for Sherith Israel, "The Remnants of Israel."
Inside Nashville's first Orthodox synagogue
with men on one side, women on the other,
the Torah scrolled center stage for readings,
Rabbi and Cantor their lead voices.
Members thrilled at a sanctum of their own—
these faithful now festive fugitives who like Houdini,
had mysteriously escaped Hungary,
a festering dot on the map.

One Yom Kippur day, folks rambled out of the Ryman
to the home next door, armed with popcorn and cheer,
enchanted with the chanting from within.
Jewish women asked fans to stay and visit,
just tossing their popcorn on this fast day.

244

Showers of greeting graced the room—
smiles on the charmed faces of both congregations,
melodies and liturgies merging in their minds,

and for a brief interval, sharing a sacred
but unexpected moment—
together.

About the Florida State Poets Association

2023–2024 FSPA OFFICERS

Mary Marcelle, President
Mark Andrew James Terry, Vice-President
Sonja Jean Craig, Secretary
Robyn Weinbaum, Treasurer

2023–2024 CERTIFIED FSPA CHAPTERS

Ancient City Poets
DeLand Boulevard Collective Poets
LGBTQIA and Friends
Live Poets Society of Daytona Beach
Miami Poets
New River Poets
North Florida Poetry Hub
Northwest Florida Poets
Orlando Area Poets
Poetry for the Love of It
South Florida Poets
Space Coast Poets
Sunshine Poets
Suncoast Writers Guild Poetry Pod
Tomoka Poets

FSPA also has many members at large who are not affiliated with a chapter. These members live not only in Florida, but in various states across the nation and countries around the globe.

NOTE: New members and chapters are welcome. Rules and requirements are on the FSPA website: www.floridastatepoetsassociation.org.

FLORIDA STATE POETS ASSOCIATION

History, Objectives, Conferences

The Florida State Poets Association, Inc. was founded in 1971 by Henrietta A. Kroah of DeLand, Florida, with the assistance of Hans Juergensen, PhD, of the University of Tampa, a past president of the National Federation of State Poetry Societies (NFSPS). Its main objective is to secure a fuller public recognition of the art of poetry, stimulate a finer and more intelligent appreciation of poetry, and to provide opportunities for the study of poetry and incentives for the writing and reading of poetry. This is accomplished through local member chapters, a bi-monthly newsletter, and multiple state contests for adults and students.

A state convention is held each October and a springtime conference is held each April.

Visit: www.floridastatepoetsassociation.org
for current events, activities, and member news

***

NATIONAL FEDERATION OF STATE POETRY SOCIETIES

NFSPS is a federation of over thirty state poetry societies. Organized in 1959 and incorporated in 1966, NFSPS provides support to the state member societies through a quarterly newsletter, various national contests, and a convention each June. Over the years FSPA members have been an integral part of the federation.

Visit: www.nfsps.com for further information

If we shadows have offended,
Think but this and all is mended:
That you have but slumbered here
While these visions did appear.
And this weak and idle theme,
No more yielding but a dream,
Gentles, do not reprehend.
If you pardon, we will mend.
And, as I am an honest Puck,
If we have unearnèd luck
Now to 'scape the serpent's tongue,
We will make amends ere long.
Else the Puck a liar call.
So good night unto you all.
Give me your hands, if we be friends,
And Robin shall restore amends.

William Shakespeare
— *A Midsummer Night's Dream, Act V*

This book created especially for you by

BAH, HUMBUG! PRODUCTIONS

Made in the USA
Coppell, TX
28 October 2024

39028568R00144